What Others Are Saying About This Book

"Strongholds such as fear, low self-esteem, guilt, broken relationships, loneliness, and habitual sin are just a few of many causes of discouragement and lack of hope. In the pages of her book, Sharon Kühn shows you that these problems are no reason to give up. She maintains that hope is always present because God is on our side.

Through promises from the Word of God and illustrations, she provides reassurance that God will help you through your struggles, also that He is our Comforter and will never abandon you. You can claim victory over discouragement and be healed of heartaches and disappointments because of God's great love for you and His plan and purpose for your life."

-- *Cliff & Verna Scott*, co-founders of *Upper Room Ministries*, Prince Albert, SK. Canada

"If you have been searching for a book which delivers what it promises, this is it. Look no further."

-- *Sylvia A. Nitz*, Author of *Inclusivism: The World on the Brink of a Social Revolution*, South Carolina, U.S.A.

"Sharon's heart to help those with deep-seated hurts shines out from the pages of this book. Having overcome her own debilitating wounds, she reaches out to help others do the same. *Fearfully and Wonderfully Made* invites you on a journey of healing and self-discovery of your God-given identity!"

-- ***Delaine Allen***, author of *Women at War*; minister and trainer for *Training for the Nations & Lifestream Ministries*; Regina, Saskatchewan, Canada

You Were Fearfully and Wonderfully Made

Discover Your True Value!

Sharon A. Kühn

WORLD WIDE
PUBLISHING GROUP

7710-T Cherry Park Dr, Ste 224
Houston, TX 77095
713-766-4272

The views expressed in this book are those of the author, and do not necessarily reflect those of the publisher.

Published in the United States of America.

Ebook: 978-3-9602-8445-1
Softcover: 978-0692624647
Hardcover: 978-1-60796-963-1

Table of Contents

Preface

The word "fearfully" in the title is the Hebrew word "yaw ray" which means to be morally revered or held in reverence.[1] It is used 334 times in the Bible. God created each of us. We are revered and held in reverence by our Creator and the hosts of heaven. Why do I say this? This Scripture pretty much sums it up –

"What is man that You are mindful of him, and the son of man that You visit him? For You have made him a little lower than the angels, and You have crowned him with glory and honor. You have made him to have dominion over the works of Your hands; You have put all things under his feet." - Psalm 8:4-6

Wrap your mind around this—"Your present circumstances do not determine where you go, but rather where you start!"

Rarely is anyone drawn to buy a book on low self-esteem or self-worth issues. Most people would go for books on diet, fitness, depression, or sleep disorders. And, maybe out of sheer curiosity, they may even consider a novel, or a do-it-yourself project book, but to opt for self-help books would be the last thing in their mind! Somewhere over the last few days, weeks or months, you have decided (or someone suggested) you need some help or at least a bit of insight to

---

[1]   E-sword, Electronic data.

help you decide whether or not you have a particular issue, which may or may not need attention.

While deciding to purchase a book*, you may do a little research on the topic, and the author, and then you will decide which one to buy. You, like everyone else, usually ask, "What makes this book different from all the others on this topic? Why was this book written, and how can it help me? Am I wasting my money and my time?"

People are always looking for ways to "feel" better about themselves and they will spend huge amounts of money searching for the answer to their personal dilemma. These people have made the self-help business a multi-million dollars a year industry.

Whatever may be the case today, God has the perfect remedy for poor or low self-worth issues and life modifications. The answer is not in a formula, but a person. God has given Himself to mankind in the person of the Holy Spirit who indwells those who have a personal relationship with Him. The Spirit then works in us to change our behavior and our self-image from the inside out.

When we accept Jesus and His Spirit, we receive the "power" and complete source for behavioral modifications and freedom from toxic thinking and lifestyle.

It is He who gives us power to change and the tools (His Word) with which to do it.

*Reading this book will do nothing for you unless you make the quality decision to put into practice God's

Scriptural prescriptions. Nothing changes unless we determine to change our thoughts, our actions and our attitudes.

From my perspective, I truly believe this book can and will help you if you put into practice the principles contained here. These are many of the same principles I had to embrace when God took me on my healing journey many years ago.

The one thing I want everyone to take away from this experience is "**how valuable, important and unique you are to the One who created you!**"

After some 20 years of watching and hearing about countless number of people, men, women and young people succumb to depression, unhealthy thoughts, self-destructive lifestyles and ultimately suicide, I could no longer stay quiet, having had some of these same thoughts pass through my mind during my thirty-plus years of hellish experience (age 9 to 40). I feel compelled to make a difference by sharing my own experience. Things that worked for me and things that did not, may or may not work for you, but at least give it a genuine go! It will depend on how serious you are about making changes in your life, which will inevitably change the outcome of how you feel about yourself and how you will deal with, react to and interact with others, especially those whom you love and those who **care about you.**

I promise you that if you take the Prayer and Word prescriptions in this book seriously, the Lord will make a way for you when there seems to be no way.

"Behold, I will do a new thing, now it shall spring forth; shall you not know it? I will even make a road in the wilderness and rivers in the desert." -Isaiah 43:19

Spaces for notes have been incorporated in this manual to provide you with an opportunity to make notes and to write down inspired ideas and thoughts that may come to your mind as the Holy Spirit leads you.

All scripture references (unless otherwise stated) are taken from the NKJV of the Holy Bible, Thomas Nelson, Inc. 1982

NOTES

Introduction
Putting Your Best Foot Forward
Recognizing the need and then desiring to act on and make the necessary change(s)

When anyone takes their own life, it has adverse effects on those left behind. When a celebrity takes his or her own life, it seems to affect society in an extremely negative and unhealthy way. What I mean by this could be understood from this scenario (a true story) – a mom came home early from work and walked in on her teenage son preparing to take his life by hanging himself. Naturally, she was horrified and when she got her thoughts together enough to ask the question, "why," his answer was, "it was the answer for so-and-so, they did it, now they don't have any more problems!" Praise God that with HIS help and the help of family, friends and professionals, this family can now celebrate their victory as to timely intervention, which they had by divine providence that day. How many folks don't get that second chance? Little do they realize the devastation they leave behind, the example they have set and the doors they have opened to even more demonic activity in the lives of those left behind.

What may seem good for the famous is definitely not always good for the average person struggling with every day issues. These celebrities spend enormous amounts of money and surround themselves with people who do their very best to make the rich and famous look like they have it altogether. If you had a chance to speak with many of them, you would hear a different story. Fame and fortune can't always buy you what is best for you. It cannot buy you love, or a good name. We are so influenced by Hollywood and media, we can scarcely tell the difference between reality and fantasy anymore; it's a slippery slope going nowhere, my friends. (I've been there and done that).

From the age of nine years to around forty, I lived with a horrible secret, afraid to tell anyone because, *first*, the fear instilled in me and then because of what others might think of me if they knew, and finally from a spirit of un-forgiveness and offense ruled by a spirit of revenge and anger (hatred). My continual cycle of thoughts were, how could "anyone" possibly understand how I felt, how can anyone love me and accept me, and why would anyone want to be my friend? All of these brought about self-doubt that gradually became a stronghold in my life.

I allowed this experience to determine thoughts and actions that shaped my life for over 30 years. To survive, I lived totally in a fantasy world (real life hurt too much, I was controlled by my thoughts and emotions, I just changed my thoughts and actions to suit my perception of the way the world I had created and learned to live and cope in rolled around), all was a fabrication of my imagination, yet with real people in it, people with feelings just like I had. I didn't care. I determined to use before I was used, was I delusional! I became an expert at hiding the real *me*. So good in fact that I even lost sight of who I was as a person. I always found myself trying to live up to what I assumed were other people's expectations of what and who I should be. No one ever suspected the battle I fought every day. I destroyed relationship after relationship, because I didn't believe anyone could really and truly care for me. The minute anyone got too close, I began my agenda of how to get out of the relationship. I left a lot of hurting and confused people in my wake. Because when cornered, I couldn't explain what I was feeling, why I was doing what I did. Then of course, just behind the screen of deception was this niggling little thought, "I am not that kind of person!"

Yet God knew! I am so thankful for HIS intervention. He slowly began to draw forth the person inside, the one who had been hidden for so long trying to protect herself and her vulnerability. I had a difficult time adjusting to what He was showing me, only used to living in my box. I think I realized just how small the box I had created to protect me had become, when suddenly with the start of each new day, I began running into the walls. I began to feel like I was suffocating, struggling to breathe. Every time I would try to figure things out, exhausting every logical (to me) and reasonable (to me) explanation as to what I should do, or how I should approach the next step, and I would dig myself deeper and deeper into despair. Then the doors to the world of imagination would open wide. Of course, I was too proud to ask for help, let alone receive it. I kept walking in pride, believing I was capable of getting a handle on whatever it was that was assaulting my mind and image of who I was. I really thought I had it all together. I allowed the demons of fear, lying and deception to begin to run riot in the attic of my mind, occupying rent free! Eventually, these feelings overflowed into my heart with bitterness and rejection, not only of myself, but of everyone who even attempted to get close to me. I couldn't see myself as worthy so why should anyone else, thus I continued a life of fantasy living, pretending I was something I was not and actually living out the hell I thought I deserved because of what happened to me. In some way, I thought I WAS RESPONSIBLE. But continuing in the charade, I was! I knew I couldn't do it alone and needed help. The biggest delusion was the fact that I thought I was so okay that I got certification as a counsellor and really thought I knew enough to help others gain control of their lives. Big no, no!

Jesus answered and said, "with men this is impossible, but with God all things are possible." Matthew 19:26

One day, I had a personal encounter with Jesus Christ, the Son of the Living God (you need to understand, I had given my life over to Him in 1971, but there was never any fruit, thoughts would begin to bombard me of "how could He love me after the things I had done, the things I'd thought, and what was done to me?" But *this time was different*, He showed me that HE did love me in a tangible way and that I was valuable and important to HIM, and that HE wanted to give me a better way of living, to give back some of those thirty-one years that were stolen from me by the enemy (the Lord helps us to redeem time) through my thoughts and ultimately the decisions and choices I made based on my toxic thinking.

16

How did this happen? The Holy Spirit moved upon my life, because some awesome friends and a faith-filled Aunt never stopped praying for me; and I began to be drawn and transformed and my mind was being renewed by the power in the Word of God. <u>As I began to read the Bible</u>, I wanted, and yearned for more, I actually hungered for the spiritual food coming from those pages, a craving was ignited in me that only He could fill.

I know that the Lord will use the information in these pages to also draw you, out of the hell you have been living for far too long, toward HIM for a renewed life in HIM. Amen.

The changes that have been wrought in me over the last 30 years, some subtle and others not quite so are a testimony to God's faithfulness and grace and mercy to me and to everyone who calls on the name of Jesus. There is not one thing I could do to earn it, buy it, or even deserve it, but He did it anyway - I could never repay the debt I owed. But I surely can share the wonderful life I now have in HIM – breaking others free from the stronghold of the enemy and inviting them into a fulfilling life in Christ. I owe it all to Jesus. I am free, free, and free. Praise Him. I just got on my knees one fateful day and cried out His name. My secret, sexual abuse!

I pray this prayer over you as you begin your journey:

Father, in Jesus' name, I thank You, that the person(s) reading this book will prosper and be in good health even as their soul(s) prosper. Lord, I call each beautiful person into

Your kingdom that they may begin to see they have the mind of Christ, and hold the thoughts of Jesus' heart. Thank You, Father, that they would put their trust in You and they would not lean unto their own understanding, but in all of their ways, acknowledge You and allow You to direct their paths.

Today, as they submit themselves to Your Word, which exposes, judges and analyzes their very thoughts and the purposes of their hearts, (For the weapons of their warfare are not carnal, but mighty through You to pulling down strongholds–intimidations, fears, doubts, unbelief and failure) I declare that they will refute arguments and theories and reasoning and every proud and lofty thing that sets (exalts) itself against the true knowledge of God; and I declare that they will lead every thought and purpose away captive into the obedience of Christ Jesus.

Lord, I come before You, and thank You that they shall be transformed by the renewing of their minds, that they may prove what is that good and acceptable and perfect will of Yours. That they will come to understand and have no fear that any weapon formed against them would prosper. For Your Word says, those who wait on the Lord shall renew their strength, they shall mount up with wings like eagles, they shall walk and not grow weary and they shall run and not faint.

Today, Father, as they commit to doing something about their circumstances that they would roll all of their worries, anxieties and cares upon You and steadfastly rely on, trust in and have faith in You, Lord God. Amen and Amen. In Jesus' name we declare it is so.

There will be other prayers and declarations throughout this writing to guide and encourage you as you journey to a better, healthier and radiant you. Sunbathe in the light of the knowledge that you are beloved of the Lord and heir to all He has to offer you through Jesus Christ. If you don't know Jesus as Lord and Savior, I encourage you to go to the end of this book and find the invitation prayer and commit yourself to a new life in Christ. Believe that He was, and is and is to come and that HE has a new life just waiting for you to embrace. You just have to want it enough to ask for it. He is a rewarder of ALL who diligently seek Him.

NOTES

I declare …

"…I am created in the image of the fairest One of all!"

He is the fairest of ten thousand…Song of Solomon 5:10

I am God's handiwork, created in Christ Jesus…
Ephesians 2:10

Acknowledgments

First and foremost, I must thank my Lord and Savior, Jesus Christ for giving me a new lease on life. Without the Holy Spirit in my life, changing me more and more into the image of God's Son, I would not be here today. I would have continued living a life of self-destruction on my way to nowhere. And, I would not have had the compulsion to write this book. I am a daughter of the King! Thank you to my wonderful husband, Edwin, who has been an encourager and next to my Lord, the most stable thing in my life, he never changes. I also need to thank my children, Glenn and Alana for always being the bright spots in my life, their lives declaring that I did do some things right back in those days. I am so proud of the awesome people you have become, knowing who upholds you with HIS right hand of grace. I love you very much.

Also a huge thank you to my Mom, Alice and my sister, Judy for never actually throwing me out of their home when I would come to share what I believed about the freedom I found in a life turned to Jesus Christ. They both now love and serve our Lord. Love is the answer, not the feeling or the emotion, but a quality decision to make a life-long commitment to one another. Thank you all for your unending and enduring love and your forgiveness and grace towards me. Also thank you to those of you that have never stopped praying for me. I love you all.

A very special thanks to two of the most creative people that I am privileged to call friends, Brent Gerlach, creator of *Restore and Design*, for his awesome cover design and inside photo and for Donna Barr, my special encouragement and example. Donna and Brent, I love you. To everyone who took the time to read through and give the much needed advice in the preliminary stages, I could not have done it without you.

And a lasting thank you to the following ladies, Mae, Naomi, Marcy and Sandra who are the inspiration I needed to finish this work. They are living testimonies on how they used the scriptures and made lasting changes in their lives.

I am not where I need to be, yet, but I am not where I used to be. Praise The Lord! Looking back on the last several years, for the most part, I have enjoyed the ride, even with its challenges, its trials and tribulations. I wouldn't go back to my old life for anything - God has delivered me from my past. He is truly the author and finisher of my faith. And He is faithful to stretch me.

An extremely heartfelt thank you to Eddie and his staff at Worldwide Publishing Group for their patience and super advice along the journey of getting this manuscript ready for publication. I could never have done it without your expertise.

And He spoke these words..."If you abide in My word...you shall know the truth, and the truth shall make you free." - John 8:30, 31, 32

"If you hear the truth, will you believe it?"

-Paula Black[2]

"You cannot dress for your future while being wrapped in the regrets and disappointments of your past."

-Bishop La Donna Osborn[3]

[2]   Paula Black, *Life, Cancer and God;* Black Eagle Publishing, Hemet, California, 2014

[3]   Bishop La Donna Osborn, June 23rd, 2015 Facebook Post; permission granted.

Chapter One
By Great Design

You are a one-of-a-kind, Masterpiece,

the work of "The Master"

"I praise You, for I am fearfully and wonderfully made. Wonderful are Your works; my soul knows it very well." –Psalm 139:14

"Before I formed you in the womb I knew you; before you were born I sanctified you; I ordained you a prophet to the nations." – Jeremiah 1:5

"…even as He chose us in Him before the foundations of the world, that we should be holy and blameless before Him, in love He predestined us for adoption as sons and daughters through Jesus Christ, according to the purpose of His will." - Ephesians 1:4-5

By a great design, and as part of a purposeful plan, you were carefully thought out from the beginning of time. You were designed with a purpose and for a particular reason and brought forth in a particular season. There is not another one like you!

If you are new to the Word of God, or someone that doesn't know the Lord at all, or you may even think of yourself as a seasoned Christian, this may seem like a lot of Scripture to process, but it is necessary to lay a good foundation for this book. And also for you to know that,

"...the gospel is the power of God unto salvation for everyone who believes..." -Romans 1:16

And

"whoever builds his/her house on the rock, it will stand but whoever builds on sand, know that in the storm it will fall and great will be its fall."

- paraphrased from Matthew 7:24-27

There is something in this book for everyone. May the Lord use it to bless, guide, encourage and transform you. For it says, God's Word is

"life to those that find them, and health to all their flesh." – Proverbs 4:22.

And, "That there may be healing to your flesh and fatness to your bones..." Proverbs 3:8.

"For I know the thoughts that I think toward you, says the Lord, thoughts of peace and not evil, to give you a future and a <u>hope</u>." – Jeremiah 29:11

Every cell, every nerve, every detail of your being was known to the One who created you, long before the creation of heaven and earth, as they say, "before you were even a twinkle in your Daddy's eye!"

You have worth and you are valuable. How valuable? So much so that God sent His only begotten Son to die for YOU! He took your place to satisfy God's perfect justice. So our sin debt - yours and mine - could be paid in full!

From the beginning of time, there has been someone who is jealous of you, someone who wants what you have and will stop at nothing to get it! He will destroy you if you let him. **That someone is Satan!** Thanks be to God for the devil's defeat at Calvary. The only battleground left for him is your *mind*. And how much access you allow and what ground you give up will determine your fate - victory or defeat. Make a firm decision right now not to rent out to Satan any space in your head.

There has been an agenda (which comes in many forms and through just as many avenues) to destroy *that* truth once you hear and recognize it (or making sure you never hear the truth) in the lives of people, and this mischief of the devil started as far back as the Garden. One of these avenues is through people, the devil will use even those close to us to destroy us if he can. The enemy (Satan) is the biggest identity thief going to and fro on earth. His whole campaign has been and always will be, (till he is taken away completely, and that time is coming soon), is to plant doubt as to the authenticity of God's Word and the Truth therein, making sure you never find out who you are in Christ Jesus, and what authority you have been given in His name – and your past does not even define who you are. The finished work of the cross defines who you are! Think about this--- YOU ARE A BRAND NEW CREATION NEVER BEFORE MADE IF YOU MAKE JESUS LORD OVER YOUR LIFE!

When the devil has you convinced you are unworthy of love, (especially God's), you will never learn to accept the truth about how much God really loves you and how precious and valuable you are to HIM.

Typically, most people with low self-worth feel and think they are unlovable, they aren't good at anything, that they just don't fit in, and will never amount to anything. Persons who struggle with self-worth issues tend to have struggles with accepting themselves for who they really are. They are the most critical of themselves and are their own biggest discouragers. To understand this, you must ask for and receive a revelation of the truth of how much HE (God) loves you and what HE (God) has done so you can have a restored relationship with HIM (God) again. Let the revelation sink deeply into your heart and out of this will come an understanding and a new appreciation of who you are and how important your place is in the family of God. You were put on this earth for a purpose. Find out what that is and go for it!

"Therefore, if anyone is in Christ, he/she is a new creation; old things have passed away; behold all things have become new." – 2 Corinthians 5:17

The devil knows he can't have any effect on you when you realize *who(se)* you are. When you accept Jesus as Lord, and His Holy Spirit (The Holy Spirit is the same power that raised Christ from the dead) comes to dwell inside of you, you will be secure and free to be yourself. The Bible says you become a new creation and it's...

"Christ in you, the hope of glory." - Colossians 1:27

which gives you the power to become a victorious overcomer. Paul writes in Romans 8:37, "Yet in all these things we are more than conquerors through Him who loved us." To be a conqueror means to fight a battle and win, but to be "more" than a conqueror means to win a battle without having to fight. Jesus fought and is still fighting on our behalf; He does it in you and through you.

Satan hates and will stop at nothing to take your focus off of that revelation, he will literally steal your identity and leave you empty and broken, or worse, dead. He will continue to attack you every chance he gets and, if possible, disarm you because it is the image and likeness of Jesus you are becoming that he hates and wants to destroy. HE HATES JESUS! And you and I were created in that image and likeness.

"eye has not seen, nor has ear heard the things that He (God) has stored up for those who believe."
-1 Corinthians 2:9

Your best defense is getting into the Scripture (the Bible) and *doing* what it says.

Ephesians 6:12-18 talks about the battle we face as sons and daughters of the Most High and it commands us to put on the whole armor of God, so that the enemy can't get to us, "For we do not wrestle against flesh and blood, but against principalities, against powers, against the rulers of the darkness of this age, against spiritual hosts of wickedness in the heavenly places. Therefore take up the <u>whole armor</u> of God, so you may be able to withstand in that evil day, and having done all, to stand. Stand, therefore, having girded your waist with the <u>belt of truth</u>, having put on the <u>breastplate</u> of <u>righteousness</u>, and having <u>shod your feet</u> with the <u>preparation</u> of the <u>gospel of peace</u>, above all, taking the <u>shield</u> of <u>faith</u> with which you will be able to quench all the fiery darts of the wicked one. And take the <u>helmet</u> of <u>salvation</u> and the <u>sword of the Spirit</u>, which is the Word of God; <u>praying always</u> with all prayer and supplication in the Spirit, being watchful to this end with all perseverance and supplication for all the saints" *

Note* I will go through the basic definition of each piece of the armor later in the book and how to use it.

"I beseech you, therefore, brethren, by the mercies of God that you present your bodies a living sacrifice, holy and acceptable to God, which is your reasonable service. And do not be conformed to this world, but be transformed by the renewing of your mind, that you may prove what is that good and acceptable and perfect will of God." - Romans 12:1-2

Too many of you have believed the lie that looking after your bodies is not important. That once or twice of something that isn't good for us won't hurt. Think again. Everything we do, EVERYTHING, every thought we have, EVERYONE eventually affects some part of you and your future. Every word you speak will have its own consequences in the physical realm. Sow good seed!

How can you make changes to your way of thinking and speaking that will assist in the positive thoughts and actions to start happening?

"So then faith comes by hearing (an acting on), and hearing by the word of God," -Romans 10:17

We are sanctified and cleansed with the washing of water by the Word of God, (Ephesians 5:26). This is saying that if you continue to *read* **and** *apply* the truths from the Bible, it will transform you into the exact image of God's Son, Jesus. The Word of God is powerful and alive and wherever it is sent, it accomplishes what it is sent to do, it never returns to God void and unproductive. Hebrews 12:4 and Isaiah 55:11.

You are probably asking, how on earth God's Word can still be alive and active? When you release it by speaking it into situations, it is activated and begins to perform what it is sent out to accomplish.

It saddens my heart to know that there are many in today's society, in the past and those of the future who will run their course in life, believing they are worthless failures, a burden on society, not realizing that this is a total and complete lie. I aim to change that.

Many, many beautiful people have decided that the world would be a better place without them and therefore make the fatal decision to end their lives abruptly and sadly, without realizing the pain and devastation this act leaves in their wake. By this act alone, you have just transferred your hell into the lives of those around you.

Suicide is a (pre-meditated) act, not only thought out, but planned by persons with low self-esteem or self-worth issues. It also includes a high percentage of people who can't or won't face the struggles of life, death of children and or spouse or loved one, loss of jobs, negative Dr. reports, and the list goes on. They have been taught to believe another lie, propagated by the devil, that they are not responsible for anything that goes wrong in their lives. They are never made to be accountable for decisions they have made and so when they run into that proverbial wall a couple times, they look for what they consider to be the easy way out. **NOT!**

All of this nastiness starts with a thought. Do you just let your thoughts control you or do you take them captive and bring them into subjection?

"But each one is tempted when he/she is drawn away by his/her own desires and enticed. Then, when desire has conceived, it gives birth to sin; and sin, when it is full-grown, brings forth death, do not be deceived, my beloved friends." - James 1:14-16

Being forewarned is being fore-armed;

"For the weapons of our warfare are not carnal but mighty in God for pulling down strongholds, casting down arguments and every high thing that exalts itself against the knowledge of God, bringing every thought into captivity to the obedience of Christ." - 2 Corinthians 10:4-5

I will say it many times throughout this book as a reminder to you who are committed to making a change for the better in your lives. Realize your battle is 100% in your own mind, so don't allow toxic thoughts to occupy mental space in your head, rent free! THEY WILL steal from you, they will destroy you and they WILL kill you!

The favored weapons of the voice in your head are toxic and they include; frustration and discouragement, doubt and unbelief, which when mixed together and left unchecked become depression. Depression leads to medications and sooner or later, this leads to dependency and more depression. The answer is not learning just to deal with them but to eliminate them completely and this is going to be the toughest part of your journey. Rejoice and be glad for Jesus has overcome all of these things and has your answers ready for you. He has your back, so to speak.

> *"No temptation has overtaken except such as is common to man; but God is faithful, who will not allow you to be tempted beyond what you are able, but with the temptation will also make the way of escape, that you may be able to bear it."*
> *- 1 Corinthians 10:13*

But, and there is always a "but". But, *love* teaches us to see ourselves and all those around us in the same way as the Lord does, as valuable individuals, each with unique gifts and talents to use for HIS glory and the furtherance of HIS kingdom. HIS kingdom will come on earth as it is in heaven, wow, through yielded vessels; that is a revelation all of its own, you don't have to wait to experience God's kingdom after you have passed into eternity, but you can begin to enjoy it here and now. My friends, there is always hope when Jesus is in the equation. He never leaves us or forsakes us, He sticks closer than a brother.

Please give this an honest go, (I really believe that if you got this far, you intend to go the whole way, congratulations) because until you recognize your worth and learn to love the person HE created you to be, you will always struggle with the image that the world has placed on you instead of the image GOD made you to be.

After each chapter I will place a prayer of declaration, where you will insert your own name in the blank and pray from a position of victory and triumph.

I, (Your name) _____ am fearfully and wonderfully made. I am created in the image of my Lord and master, Jesus Christ. I can do all things through Christ who strengthens me for I have been given the mind of Christ. Amen.

NOTES

Chapter Two
God Don't Make No Junk!
Do you believe this?

What is your attitude? Is it one of gratitude, or is it one of whining, murmuring and complaining?

"Nope, not me, uh, uh, can't do it. Too hard, I don't even know where to start, it's no use, I've tried programs and books before, none of it works." You're RIGHT! Secular (worldly) self-help stuff out there will never work. Why? Simply put, because it isn't what God wants or has planned for you, that's why. Each of your issues will be totally different than the next person.

The first thing you must remember is that as a creation of the Living God, you and I are created like no other thing, in that we were given the right to choose, no one has the power to make you or I do anything we do not choose or want to do, to think the things we don't want to think and to speak the things we don't want to speak.

Argue or disagree all you like, how has what you have been doing and believing been working for you up until now? How have the talk show hosts helped you? Likely as not they have left you feeling even more confused after a couple weeks or months and lower than before you heard them. And a few bucks poorer. The highs they promise are only short-lived and then you are on another circle, going nowhere. THERE ARE NO INSTANT FIXES! "Instant" does not accomplish what is needed for us to change. It is in these trials and tribulations that we are made perfect.

"And not only that, but we also glory in tribulations, knowing that tribulation produces perseverance; perseverance, character; and character, hope."
- Romans 5:3-5

"by which have been given to us exceedingly great and precious promises, that through these you may be partakers of the divine nature, having escaped the corruptions that is in the world through lust. But also for this very reason, giving all diligence, add to your faith virtue, to virtue knowledge, to knowledge self-control, to self-control perseverance, to perseverance godliness and to godliness brotherly kindness and to brotherly kindness, love." **- 2 Peter 1:4-7**

Secondly, *I can't do it for you,* no one can, you are the only one who can acknowledge that you have a stinking attitude and it's time to change that. Good advice to anyone reading this with motivation to see change happen for you – "don't let anyone or anything that is not for your wholeness RENT space between your ears!

Yes, I know that I didn't experience your childhood, your marriage, your job and co-workers, your relatives or your neighbors, but, it is high time you let go of those excuses and decided you are going to take a stand. You must realize that you must become responsible for your life, attitude and actions, you are going to become accountable for your choices!

Is it going to be easy? **NO!** If you stick with it, is it going to be worth it? **YES!** Will you always get it right, **NO**, but that doesn't give you the right to quit. My friends, quitting is not an option in the game of life. You only get one crack at it! So...let's get started ...get yourself a Bible with a good Concordance...a pen and LOTS and LOTS of paper. There is something therapeutic about writing stuff down. It helps you to recognize the things that need addressing and to see step by step the changes that are taking place even if you don't notice them at first. This is going to be the ride of your life, for better and not worse, so you might as well decide right now you are going to enjoy the journey.

Why the Bible? Firstly, because I don't pretend to have all the answers and secondly, because what you are going to learn is from the One who made you, and He will show you exactly who you are, how valuable you really are, and how much He loves you and that HE is the only one who knows exactly what it is going to take to fix you. I am just the vessel through whom HE has chosen to speak at this time into your life, nothing more or less.

We do it God's way and no other way. You need to make a decision right now and that is, you will trust, believe and act on the promises of God and you will not turn to the left or the right. Bad attitudes, bad habits and wrong thinking are formed over time, they do not just pop up in your head overnight. It will take as long as you want it to and will be as hard as you make it. It will be a test of your faith in the supernatural.

Let me give you a quick nugget to chew on as we start,

"HE touched their eyes and said, 'be it done unto you according to your faith'" - Matthew 9:29

Be willing to admit you have an issue(s), which needs fixing, dig your heels in!

"...for all have gone astray and fall short of the glory of God," – Romans 3:23

"Do you WANT to be made well?" - John 5:6

It is entirely up to you as an individual to put the information and knowledge you receive into tangible action in your own situation. This is called wisdom. Take what you learn and make it work for you. Practice, practice, and practice, till it becomes second nature and you will be doing it without even thinking. The new *you* will begin to make the proper decisions and right choices for you and your situation based on what God says about you and not on what people say about you.

Another asset to your pen and paper will be a hand-held mirror. Yes, that's what I said, a hand-held mirror. You are going to talk to yourself every day, over and over until you get it..."You are unique, you are special and you are definitely worth it. You are loved and extremely valuable." You will learn not to look at the image in the mirror with self-rejection, but with honor and respect because you are fearfully and wonderfully made. Amen.

Pray this prayer for the conquering of your toxic thought life:

In the name of Jesus, I (Your name)_____ thank You Lord, that you are teaching me to take authority over my thought life. Even though I live in the flesh, I am not carrying on my warfare according to the flesh and using mere human weapons, for the weapons of my warfare are not physical, but they are mighty before God for the overthrow and destruction of strongholds. I will bless the Lord with every thought and purpose in my life.

I declare that my mind will not wander, with my spirit, soul and body, I will bless the Lord. I (Your name) _____ will have the mind of Christ, and will practice what I have heard and learned and seen in Christ and model His way of living, and the God of peace (untroubled, undisturbed well-being)—will be with me.

Amen

NOTES

Chapter Three

Choices, Breaking Toxic Thought Patterns

Are you ready for a fight?

"And do not be conformed to this world, but be transformed by the renewing of your mind, that you may prove what is the good and acceptable and perfect will of God." - Romans 12:2

It seems very difficult, even impossible for people to accept unconditional love – yet that is exactly what God offers you every minute of every day. Most humans cannot give what they have never experienced themselves. And, ultimately hurting people will always hurt people.

As a rule of thumb, you filter the love you get from and give to others through a critical spirit. You can't give what you have never learned to receive, what you don't believe and what you seldom understand.

Humans consistently think of love in terms of feelings, emotions and attitudes (what you were taught, what you watched day after day, and what MEDIA portrays as the truth about love). Unfortunately, a new character has come on the scene in the last few years, his name is… "What's in it for me?" Remember one thing if you don't remember anything else, LOVE IS NOT SELF-SERVING! **Love serves others!** Somewhere along life's highway we are usually programmed to believe and accept that our worth is performance-based. Media is a huge player in this deception.

Let's think about adding to our equation or journey, a couple of trusted family or friends to hold us up when it seems like nobody cares. (This is optional and your choice, but helps make it easier and will help your success especially if you are held accountable).

You may want to turn this adventure into a girl's morning coffee, or an afternoon tea or an evening with trusted friends. If you know someone else who needs to see their self as relevant, intelligent and worthy, invite that person to join your journey and together you can encourage and be accountable to each other to keep you both headed in the right direction. Choose someone who will be able to correct and encourage in a spirit of love, and who understands what it means to be confidential.

"Your word I have hidden in my heart, that I might not sin against You." - Psalm 119:11

The Bible encourages you to put away unwholesome living, but unless your mind is renewed, this is practically impossible.

Remember what I said about the enemy of your soul, the one who wants to steal your identity? My friend, guaranteed, he will stop at nothing! I am not kidding! And I am here to help you, the only way I know how and that is to first help you identify and destroy the lies, (and introduce you to the all-time healer and rewarder of those who diligently seek HIM). I want to help you discard the lies you so helplessly and hopelessly believe about yourself. You must do away with those lies formed in your thought process by <u>outside influence</u> and then those that were formed on the <u>inside by your own choices</u>. Prayerfully I wish to help you build a new attitude about the "new you" by faith.

All of us hear voice(s) in our heads. And, as part of the process, we must begin to recognize whether or not they are for us or against us. Once we have established whether they are good or evil, then we can and will begin to build up the good ones and remove the evil ones. God never puts us down, God never puts guilt or condemnation on anyone. He loves, encourages and edifies. The toxic thoughts come from only one place, the enemy of our souls, the devil, who is a liar from the beginning and the father of all lies.

> *"I call heaven and earth as witnesses against you, that I have set before you life and death, blessing and cursing; <u>THEREFORE</u> choose life, that both you and your descendants may live..." -Deuteronomy 30:19*

God has given us the gift of making our own choices, this has been proven not only in Scripture but in science as well. Research argues against the fact that we are genetically controlled, this includes behavior and emotions. So with that said, it only stands to reason that we are not, nor have ever been, the victim of our biology.[4]

---

[4]   Dispenza, "Evolve Your Brain"; Doidge, <u>The Brain That Changes Itself</u>; Freeman, <u>The societies of Brains</u>; Pert, <u>Molecules of Emotion</u>

What this means is obvious, we must take responsibility for our own choices and the words, actions and behavior that accompany them. What I am trying to say is this: according to these men and women of science, we can switch our behavioral and emotional genes on and off by the choices we make. God created humans with the freewill to make choices; and in His covenant with mankind also, He cannot over-ride our choice because of His forthright character. He never ever breaks a promise.

Admittedly, it will be difficult to recognize all the toxic thoughts at once. Thoughts which contribute to the image you have of yourself and those that bombard you every day. Thoughts that help shape the lies and give strength to them, or thoughts that help to identify the negative emotions in you. As you begin to embrace good thoughts about who you are based on God's Word and dwell on the truth therein, you will begin to replace those lies with strong, encouraging and comforting words of truth and edification. PLEASE REMEMBER YOUR EMOTIONS ARE FICKLE AND THEY NEED TO BE PUT IN THEIR PLACE. Your emotions are not your friends on this ride. You need to begin to believe the things God says about you, because that is the way He made you!

While on this journey, you may want to park your emotions, your feelings, outside in the hallway, as a belligerent, uncooperative, spoiled child that doesn't get their way every time! If you are not tough on your feelings, I will guarantee that they will derail you along the way. As long as you allow your feelings to rule your thoughts, they won't let you get to chapter four. Decide to take a stand, right now!

Begin by taking a few minutes to ask for guidance from the Holy Spirit. Pray that you will not give in to temptation and distraction; second, decide right from the start that it is GOD'S WILL and not your own that you will follow. Thank HIM for the answers to your prayers and praise HIM for HIS faithfulness to see you through this time even before you see any changes in the natural, physical realm. Will you fail some days? YES, OF COURSE! Is it the end of the world? NO! Be on guard against physical and mental distractions, self-pity, and negative thoughts. Remember that most of what you are experiencing in your life today is from your feelings getting in the way. Lack of sleep, exercise and an improper diet are huge contributors to your mental state.

"For a righteous man may fall seven times and rise again..." - Proverbs 24:16

God will never let you stay down if you are honest and truly seeking change in your circumstances.

Let's begin with the strongest three thoughts that present themselves regularly. They may be guilt, doubt, or a combination of both. They may be feelings of frustration, condemnation or depression. You may have issues with your looks, your weight, your lot in life, your job, your kids, your finances, even your spouse. It could just be an unshakable feeling of blah, (let me caution you here, that sometimes we are just lazy about having to make important life-altering choices, so we let things slide and pile up till we get caught in the cycle of "there's too much to do" or "think about" and thus we just won't do anything today), and as a result, your mountain gets bigger and bigger, and soon what was a molehill is now too high to climb. Watch out, if left unresolved, this will ultimately overcome and overwhelm you and cause you to want to lay down and give up. **Do something,** even if it's just brushing your teeth, combing your hair, getting the mail. These circumstances will be different for everyone.

Don't worry about how bad, how silly or how disgusting the negative thoughts are. Above all, be HONEST. Remember you and GOD are the only one who knows the truth about your thoughts, always remember what you have experienced is not exclusive to you, you are not the only one having these thoughts, others have experienced what you are experiencing and have overcome and now have the ability to help you, if you will open up and let them.

Read through the following examples of situations, some may even be what you are facing or someone you know may be having these issues. Keys to remember: you are not the only one who has lived in a physically abusive relationship, you are not the only one who has survived sexual abuse, and you will not be the first or the last to be at the receiving end of verbal abuse. You are not the only one who has ever experienced being bullied, and you most certainly are not the only one living with an addiction or the results of someone else's addiction(s). You are not the only one who has lived through foster care, abusive parents or teachers and coaches. My friend, you are not the only one living with financial woes. All of these things have been going on as long as there have been people on the planet, since Adam and Eve chose to disobey God. That is not to say that they are okay or acceptable. Too many think that they are the only one going through a particular situation and therefore are afraid to share their feelings and thoughts because of what others may think of them. What God thinks is all that matters at this moment in time. Remember that!

Write down on a piece of paper (journal, journal, journal) in order of their significance the most toxic thoughts that plague you frequently. Slowly you will begin to see what thoughts create what actions and subsequent thoughts and actions. By applying the technique of speaking to your mountain, you will start to deal effectively with them by using the guide I am giving you. This process will work for you, and most people, in destroying the destructive hold that *your* negative thoughts already have on you. You CANNOT change other people's way of thinking! Just your own!

As I begin to walk you through how to deal with them, keep making notes (journal) throughout the journey you have so bravely embarked on. You will need your notes, go back on them as often as you need to see patterns. It may take several times, just to show you how far you have come. You will be replacing the negative thoughts with positive ones, based on Scriptures, thoughts you are now learning about who you really are and how to use them to counteract the enemy's battle and therefore forcing him to lose his grip on your soul, eventually letting go and completely removing this poison from your mind. Once you have successfully been able to take a particular area into captivity and write the positive message beside the old way of thinking, you can destroy the paper it was written on, you can burn it, flush it, throw it out, doesn't matter. You may even choose to keep the notes for reflection at some later date. Be patient with yourself. For the time being, you are going to move from one thought to the next, and you will keep doing it until you have a whole new perspective of who you are. Some of you will be able to move over more than one thought at a time, be careful that you don't use this as a way to try to circumvent the time and healing process required to make you choose wisely, to make you love yourself and others more, to allow yourself time to become whole. Change is never easy. God will never leave you alone to do this. Habits of all kinds take 21-day cycles to establish, to remove or change.

Here is the primary reason for a Bible and good concordance. In the examples below, you will see some of the issues such as, *"not feeling loved"* or *"feeling misunderstood"*, or *"lonely"*, or *"feeling ugly"*! You will be taking the concordance and looking up the words and thought references and finding the corresponding scriptures till you find the most appropriate one wherein you believe God is personally speaking to you.

Then what, you ask? Meditate on it. Read it. Memorize it. Write it out. Act it. Speak it out loud to yourself, using your mirror or a friend until it becomes so real on the inside of you that you want to jump out of your skin. Will this frustrate you, of course it will. Keep doing it, until a new image is birthed on the inside of you. So when the thought of unworthiness comes into your mind you can say, uh, uh, you move over cause this is what God says about me,

"I have been chosen by God and am called Holy and Beloved." - paraphrase of Colossians 3:12

A word of exhortation: Your thoughts are the essence of who you are, but how you react to them and others around you (primarily with the words of YOUR mouth*) will determine how successful you will be with this project. Scripture says, "Out of the abundance of the heart, the MOUTH speaks." So what is in your heart that has to change and change quickly? How you speak about yourself and others will be the key to your breakthrough. This is why we must begin to fill our hearts with the promises and will of God for our life, so that when we are facing the lion's den, we will speak words of comfort, encouragement, uplifting and edifying, correction.

When David faced Goliath, he was prepared by his experience with God in previous situations, his comment was, "the Lord has delivered me from the paw of the bear and the lion, He will deliver me from this uncircumcised Philistine as well."

You too will be delivered from your enemies if you put your trust in God!

*Note: there is a prayer at the end of this book that deals with the words of our mouths.

Example #1 – The thought comes into your mind that nobody loves you or understands you, you are alone in this world and nobody cares about you, so what is the use of even trying. You will just do what you want, when you want, how you want and damn the consequences!*

*Note: for every action, there is a corresponding reaction. In other words, everything you choose to do will have a consequence, for either good or bad. A key here is to remember that what you are going through is not necessarily the problem, but how you are reacting to what you are going through, has lasting effects.

As an example, you will look up the terms *lonely*, *misunderstood*, and *unlovable* in the concordance and pick one verse that best addresses your issue:

For instance, you can counteract that thought with this verse from **Jeremiah 31:3-4a,**

> *"The Lord has appeared of old to me, saying, 'Yes, I have LOVED you with an everlasting love; therefore with loving-kindness I have drawn you. Again I will build you and you shall be rebuilt.'"*

Example #2 - I can't do this alone, there is no one to help me. I am by myself. Nobody understands.

Replace that thought with this: **Isaiah 41:10**.

"I have chosen you and have not cast you away; Fear not, for I AM with you; be not dismayed, for I AM your God. I will strengthen you, yes, I will help you, I will uphold you with my righteous right hand"

Now think about this: "are your thoughts holding you hostage or are you holding your thoughts captive?

We will look at a few more examples:

Example #3 – "Oh, no, I couldn't do that, what would people say (or think) if they knew I had an extra-marital affair? No one wants to associate with an adulteress!" Counteract it with the story from the Book of John, chapter 8. The religious leaders of the day brought a woman caught in adultery to Jesus, (you will notice they didn't bring the man) they were ready to stone her, but Jesus stood up and said to them, "The one among you without sin can throw the first stone," and HE bent and wrote on the ground. When Jesus looked up, there was no one left except the woman. He then asked her where her accusers were and if there was no one left to condemn her, she said, "no," and Jesus, Himself said, "then neither do I, go your way and do not sin anymore." He forgave her and cautioned her to not do this again. He is saying the same to you every day, I forgive you, but please don't do this again.

Jesus died such that ALL of your sins were forgiven. He asks you to come to Him and receive HIS free gift of forgiveness and salvation, then as you allow the Holy Spirit to work in and through you, you can become more and more like HIM. We can't earn it or buy it. It is there for everyone who believes and asks for it. What an awesome gift He died to give us. Glory, you and I have been forgiven, He paid the penalty of our disobedience and sin and offers us His right standing with God in exchange. Wow!

Example #4 – The toughest thought to overcome is this:

Your friend: "You should really try to _forgive_ so and so, it would help you heal" or "it would help you release the stress and maybe you just might sleep better"

You: "Yah, I think you may be right, I have carried this too far, I will call tomorrow."

The enemy of your soul speaks up as you lay in bed thinking; "Are you kidding me, how could you even consider forgiving him/her/them after what they did to you. Do I have to replay it for you again? Remember the last time you tried this, they promised and guess what happened, you can't be seriously entertaining the thought of forgiveness again? Are you that stupid to think it will ever work?"

You: "Yeah, you're right. How could I be so gullible to think that they deserve my forgiveness, never, never, never, never." You toss and turn all night going over the situation again and again. Guess who loses? You wake up lacking sleep, irritated, confused and angry, you lash out at the first person who gets in your face and the cycle starts all over again.

Counteract that thought with this:

"For if you forgive men their trespasses, your heavenly Father will also forgive you. But if you do not forgive men their trespasses, neither will your heavenly Father forgive you. - **Matthew 6:14-15**

Forgiveness is not an "if you feel like doing it" issue; but a command of our heavenly FATHER.

There will be more scripture ammunition for battle strategies in later chapters, with space to write your own as you find them.

When you serve your flesh and your desires, you are ruled by the spirits of pride and selfishness – both are instrumental in keeping you bound in jealousy, un-forgiveness, offense, bitterness – the chain keeps getting tighter the more you refuse to forgive and let it go. It keeps you from forgiving because you don't want to release the other person. NEWS FLASH! The other person is likely not even thinking about you or your issues. Forgiving is NOT for them, it is FOR YOU! Harboring un-forgiveness and offense in your life KEEPS you in BONDAGE! And eventually it will begin to rob you of your health, spiritual, mental and physical.

Beware of distractions, I can't stress this enough. While in what I call *the valley of decision*, you will face choices on every level – daily, minute by minute – and every decision you make comes with its own set or series of consequences. Good or bad, they will inevitably show up somewhere, somehow. These decisions will affect your character, and it will ultimately affect all of your relationships for good or bad. "But if you do not forgive men their trespasses, neither will your FATHER forgive you!" It will affect your health, relationships, wealth, productivity and your eternal destiny. The consequences will make you or break you and you cannot say, "But, if…or they made me…it was so-and-so's fault, I did that," no, my friend, you made a choice based on the seed in your heart, regardless of who put that seed there. Your choices are the sum total of who you are, how you see yourself, what you believe, and will initiate what you will eventually become. Are you happy with who you are? You have a choice to begin making decisions based on the goal you have set and the commitment you have made to change what nobody else can. YOU!

"Above all else, guard your heart, for everything you do flows from it." – **Proverbs 4:23**

Another translation puts it this way,

"Guard your heart above all else for it determines the course of your life." - **Proverbs 4:23**

Understand that you alone have the power by the HOLY SPIRIT to change yourself and no one else. And I am convinced that you can go the mile and succeed. This is wisdom. Always look at your choice through this prayer, deciding whether it is something you can change or something you must accept, if you can; and ask God to always give you wisdom to know the difference.

The Serenity Prayer

God grant me the Serenity to accept the things

I cannot change; the courage to change the things I can;

And the wisdom to know the difference.[5]

You can take it one step further and add this scripture;

"A good man/woman out of the good treasures stored in his/her heart brings forth good; and an evil man/woman out of the evil stores of his/her heart brings forth evil. For out of the abundance of the heart the mouth speaks." -paraphrase of **Luke 6:45**

What kind of stuff have you allowed in your heart, things that determine your attitude, your speech and your course in life? *Get rid of them!* Guard everything that has access to your eyes and ears, it will ultimately end up in your heart and then out of your mouth.

Talk the answer, not the problem!

Pray this prayer –

In the name of Jesus, I (Your name)_____ask You, to bless those who have used me. Whenever I feel afraid, I declare that You are not the author of fear. I am a child of God and am not ruled by fear. I will put my whole trust in You. When I begin to sense a feeling of misery coming over me, I will express thanksgiving; and when I feel that life is

---

5   Reinhold Niebuhr, *Serenity Prayer, 1892*.

unfair, bring to my remembrance that You are more than enough. Remind me of how much You love me and how unique I am in Your eyes.

When I feel ashamed, help me, Lord, to remember that I no longer have to be ashamed; You will not allow me to suffer shame. I am delivered from the fear of disgrace; I will not be humiliated. I relinquish the shame of my youth.

Praise You, that I am being transformed through the renewing of my mind. I am able to test and prove what is Your will - Your good and acceptable and perfect will for me as Your daughter/son. You have great and awesome things reserved for my future, all my needs are met according to Your riches in glory by Christ Jesus. I will replace my old way of thinking with the promises You have made to me in Your Word. Amen.

NOTES

Chapter Four
Actions Speak Louder Than Words

"Are you the Guinness World Book record holder of procrastination or just limited thinking?"

"For as the body without the spirit is dead, so faith without works is also dead" -James 2:26

Separating your faith from corresponding action produces a dead religion with no power. Whitewashed tombs full of dead men's bones. You can say all the right things and think all the right thoughts but if your actions don't match up with your words, you are a liar and a hypocrite.

Sometimes when you get together with others of similar natures and coping skill, you tend to get drawn up into the inevitable circus. Be extremely careful about how involved you get in other people's worldly problems and negative issues, particularly those who have no desire to be free, to be healed and whole. This is called co-dependence and if you are of the co-dependent nature, you will easily become a victim in and of their situation.

You may even have the care-giver nature which automatically puts you in a position to help (rescue) everyone you see from their problems. You can't take someone from pit to throne by rescuing them. You can help by recognizing their need and point them in the right direction. They must make the choice, just like you did. You can usually tell if they are the victim type, they live in a recurring cycle of "poor me," always the victim and never the victor. This comes from the entitlement mindset, people who are always looking for others to help (rescue) them, do it for them, never lifting a finger to do anything for himself/herself. So their victories are very short-lived and temporary.

That is why most of the world's advice on self-esteem never works, because most of the readers are looking for instant fix. You must work the plan, minute by minute, until your mind is totally renewed and your heart is full of new creation ideas.

"How can you expect to do great exploits for the kingdom if you can't get victory over a sink full of dirty dishes?"[6] Think about it.

There comes a time in everyone's life when you become totally responsible for the outcomes in it. It is no longer anyone's problem but yours! It's called growing up and becoming an adult! You have to begin to make decisions based on what you want and know instead of what others tell you. Before you react to what someone has said, make sure you are really hearing what they said and not what you think they said.

Play it over in your mind, being objective. If you have to, write it down and then re-read it tomorrow, with a clear head. Learn to think for yourself. Learn to filter everything you hear through the Word of God, not your emotions. And

---

[6]   Joyce Meyers, Bible teacher and author. Television broadcast, 2001

certainly not through your feelings of the moment, that is dangerous ground.

"A man has joy by the answer of his mouth, and a word spoken in due season, how good it is!" - **Proverbs 15:23**

"A word fitly spoken is like apples of gold in settings of silver." - **Proverbs 25:11**

Your commitment to changing your way of thinking about yourself and how others see you is all about putting into action the things you need, thoughts that will make the difference and doing them over and over till they become how you see yourself, according to who God created you to be.

He (God), can even save you from yourself, just remember He loves you even when you find it hard to love yourself. The Bible, His Word, is a complete, never fail, how to guide for every situation we face in life.

Let God's peace flow in you as a river gently flows downstream. Allow it to carry away the toxins of painful memories and hurtful circumstances. Let His Spirit bring to you a fresh and clear stream of pure life and restoring thoughts.[7]

You need to resurrect the person inside of you (the one God created for a special purpose) that is still capable of

---

[7]   Frances J. Roberts, *Come Away My Beloved,* Harbor House Publishing, 1970

dreaming big, finding the people that will encourage and keep you moving forward one step at a time.

Was Rome built in a day? NOT ON YOUR LIFE! The greatest things achieved in life are those that are worth fighting for (and sometimes it's a hard fight) every step of the way, and yes, you will get hurt along the way, you will not always win, you will not always have fun, but at least you will be ALIVE. You learn from these things and move forward. Don't stop and make camp in the middle of an issue.

Unfortunately, there are those who will not admit it, but enjoy the attention they get in the middle of their crisis and so they stay there, day in and day out, different crisis, different day, but the same pile. They are victims of their own drama. You have been designed to "go through" not around or over your mountains. Every time you go through them, you become stronger, bolder, more self-confident and more motivated. You come out with a rare breed of humility, hard to describe and a peace that defies understanding and logic. Going around your issues makes you weak, less ambitious and totally unconscious to others around you, (going around tends to have you focused on "not this again" and "why me," or asking God to remove the problem just adds to it, and it has you focused on the length of your trip and how difficult it is 24/7, not what you can take away from the experience).

Your self-image is usually formed early in your life and you base it on feedback from parents, teachers, and other authority figures, even our peers tend to look at things through the natural view and aren't much help - so changing it is never easy.

Christ empowers you to slip out of who you were forced to be and transforms you into who He created you to be.

"But as many as received Him, to them He gave the right to become children of God" - John 1:12

"Faith does not operate in the realm of the possible. There is no glory for God in that which is humanly possible. Faith begins where man's power ends."

- George Mueller[8]

"He also brought me out into a broad place; He delivered me because He delighted in me." - Psalm 18:19

Get Out of The Box[9]

A respected councilor once said, "First you crawled, then you learned to walk and the world grew bigger. Then you rode a bike...drove a car...bought a plane ticket. Suddenly the horizons were limitless. Then doubts crept in; I can't (you fill in the blank)...and your world shrank a little. I shouldn't take that trip...I'll never find my way around...I have too many responsibilities. And it shrinks a little more...

---

[8]   The Autobiography of George Mueller, Whittaker House

[9]   Bob and Debby Gass;   from The Word For You Today, UCB Broadcasting & Publishing, January, February, March 2015

(until) you're sitting in a little box with the lid tightly affixed. No experiences, no lessons, no life. Boxes can be comfortable...but no matter how cozy you make it, it's still a box. They come in all shapes and sizes. When we let unrealistic fears hold us back, we can be fairly certain we're climbing inside another box...and sooner or later we'll run into the walls. Find one small 'I can't' in your life, and take the lid off the box...try for a minor impossibility...apply for that dream job...start pursuing your vision...poke the top off your box. Stick your head out and look around. Find a fear and turn it into a ladder. Get out of the box of doubt and insecurity and into the freedom of courage and belief." End of quote.

If you let it, fear will cause your imagination to run riot. But...

"God has not given us the spirit of fear, but of power and of love and of a sound mind" **-2 Timothy 1:17**

A sound mind restores our perspective and helps us see things from God's viewpoint, where all things are possible to him who believes. Today, He wants to give us the courage to climb out of the box and bring us "into a large place," because He delights in us. Amen.

I do understand that sometimes it takes every ounce of strength, will, courage and just plain determination to put one foot in front of the other. But let me tell you that for every step you make in the right direction, your identity will become clearer and stronger, not only to you, but to those around you. As you begin to define who you are by the truth of God's word, you will gain a new perspective on your life. Your goals and dreams will suddenly become attainable again. Don't ever stop dreaming my friend. These dreams are possibly God's vision for you.

I declare that I back up my faith with corresponding action. I (Your name) _____ am a doer of the Word, not only a hearer. God's word guarantees it will be worth the effort I put into it.

NOTES

Chapter Five

Out Of The Blue, But True

Do we honor one another or do we compete
with one another?

*"Husbands love your wives, as Christ loved the
church and gave himself for her..." - Ephesians 5:25*

And...

*"Wives, respect your husbands as to the Lord..." -
Ephesians 5:22*

Many people use this Scripture to justify treating women
as doormats and rob them of their voice and right to
leadership roles. If you read the Bible well, you will notice a
few significant roles of women there! Deborah led the nation
of Israel (Judges 4). Huldah, a prophetess, spoke the Word of
God to Kings (2 Kings 22). Let us read the Scripture again:
"Wives, submit to your own husbands, as to the Lord."

As a wife, you are called to submit to "your own
husband," not to all men. In God's eyes, men and women
are equal (Galatians 3:28). Paul is not speaking about your
"person," he is speaking about your "role" in the home. As a
human being, a general is not more important than a
sergeant. But for an army to function successfully, there
must be a respected chain of command where one leads and
the other follows. God doesn't want you to squirm under
your husband's (wife's) leadership (in some cases

domination), but He intended for you to snuggle into the security that it should afford you. You can excel in your career while you still allow yourself to enjoy being nurtured, loved, and protected by your spouse.

Properly understood, your spouse's love and leadership does not rob you of your strength, it simply keeps you in balance by allowing you to reconnect with your softer side and your femininity. A word of caution: if you're looking for a man (or a woman) to be your everything, forget it! GOD is the only One who can be everything to everybody. By expecting perfection from your husband/wife, you are asking more from someone than they can ever hope to give, and much more than you can provide yourself. Here's God's plan:

> *"She/he is your equal partner in God's gift of new life. Treat her/him as you should so your prayers are not hindered"* - **1 Peter 3:7**

> *"...and the peace of God, which surpasses all understanding, will guard your hearts and minds through Christ Jesus."* - **Philippians 4:7**

It isn't about left-brain thinkers vs right-brain thinkers, or for women/men only, it has nothing to do with "X" or "Y" Chromosomes, either!

There are issues that we learn as we grow and mature, which are not indicative (serving as a sign or indication of something) of our young formative years and the influence of the parent/family. Many of the self-esteem issues faced by both genders can come from our outside influence, friends, school, media (the Big One) and culture; and believe me, none of these are in it for your welfare, but, how much money they can make off of you and your crisis, whatever that may be. We are assaulted daily by magazine covers, the ads and stories, television advertisements with the latest craze, the newest fad, the sure-fire cure, the ultimate this-that-and-the-other, guaranteed to work for you. Yada Yada!

Do you buy into it, **of course you do!** We all did! You are no different than the rest of humanity, everyone falls for these schemes more than once during our life. Our primary goal in life is to fit in and be loved and accepted. This causes you to do extremely strange things based on your choices and reactions to your circumstances, all because you just want to fit in and be loved for who you think you are.

Acceptance and love are the two things you crave and will stop at nothing to achieve. It is a nirvana (a state of perfection) that really doesn't exist separate from the way you learn to cope. It seems like you are bombarded from every side until you feel like you're spinning out of control.

One day you may wake up to an emptiness deep inside which you have tried to fill with things of the world, diets, hair-dos, drugs, cars, multiple relationships, etc. Without Jesus, you will barely exist, and no matter how hard you look, you will find nothing that can permanently satisfy this emptiness. Only Christ can give you the peace you seek, not as the world seeks but as a created being of the Most High God.

There are three or four issues where men suffer in the self-esteem area that women usually don't. A good portion of this type of thinking has evolved from the media, from the world's idea of the perfect man. These areas include finances, the ability to perform well in the workplace, in the home, and whether or not we want to admit it, in the bedroom, extremely touchy subjects, all of them. I will not be going in depth on any of these topics in this book, but it is something to keep in mind when dealing with the male gender.

My personal opinion is that as the women's movement has grown so has our emasculation of the male gender. They think and feel differently than women! You can't change that, (just imagine a world where men thought and acted like women, or visa versa. Yikes! What an experience that would be). God designed them to think like they do and women to think like they do, in this should come balance. Men and women were created to complement one another, not rule over one another or compete with each other.

As men, being honest with oneself is important because you are the only one who can identify the self-esteem issues that may plague you or someone close to you.

This is not a finger-pointing session either. It is simply to help you recognize and deal with issues that may have been depriving you or someone you know, of an elevated and healthy self-worth that you deserve or the kind of relationship you are striving for in your marriage or friendships.

This is a great place to remind yourself (both men and women) that you were designed a certain way for a certain purpose and that was not to impress females/males, with the big "truck," "the super ginormous paycheck," or even "the super 6-pack abs." Ladies, your "illusive "Barbie-doll figure" or add-ons and take-offs really don't accurately describe who you are. This, my friends, is for your egos and to impress your friends. This kind of (shallow) ego will always get you into trouble.

Ladies, "Just 'cause he doesn't feel what you do, doesn't mean he doesn't have feelings!" Be nice about his truck! Fellas, be nice about her hairdo or her outfit. But be honest!

Most women don't want to admit it, but they measure men today in the same way as men used to measure women, as a prize or an object for their satisfaction, something they have to conquer. Unfortunately, none of it has to do with the things that are important for a long-lasting and healthy relationship with one other.

"A man shall leave his father and mother and be joined to his wife, and the two shall become one flesh!" - Genesis 2:24; Matthew 19:5; Ephesians 5:31; and Mark 10:7

Again, I can't stress enough that this is not a competition, it isn't about who is right or wrong, it is definitely not about who makes the most money or whose job is more important, or even whether you can do something better than he/she can, or visa versa. And it is definitely not about doing it his way or her way. It's about doing whatever it takes to make the relationship work. We were created to become one and to complement and aid or strengthen one another, not dominate one another. This is not going to work if you are only prepared to give 50%, each of you must give 100% to making your relationships work.

It is about complementing one another, working together in harmony, not one-up-man-ship. By far the most important component of any relationship is two-way communication. Some talking, and a whole lot of listening. Don't hear through a worldview but through a God-view. That is why we have one mouth and two ears, we are to listen twice as much as we are to speak. Communication is the first and most important thing in a successful relationship.

When you become a couple, the first 'cast in stone' rule that needs to be established in your relationship is this, as a husband and wife: *your parents don't live here*, their opinions are not welcome unless solicited, and please don't ask for their opinion unless you are prepared to follow through and do what is suggested. They are not there to make any of your decisions, you are grown and should be capable of making the most basic decisions for yourself. They are no longer your lifeline, they don't pay the bills and they aren't built-in baby sitters. Getting this out of the way right off the hop will put you on a good road to success in your relationship. After all, you were mature enough to decide you wanted this relationship; now live it out. Don't argue about what channel to watch on television, go to a movie! Play a board game. Go for a walk.

I will admit this sounds a bit glib and sarcastic, but think about it. Most marriages have problems based on self-absorption, and selfishness, and finances, pure and simple.

Making a marriage work at the best of times can be a daunting experience. When you consider the blending of two totally unique personalities, two possibly different cultures, two different upbringings and backgrounds, it is amazing that God instituted marriage and expected it to work.

Marriage between one man and one woman was His idea, the two shall become one! Yet He must have known it could and should work or He wouldn't have made it part of His design. Now, add in or consider trying to blend two families after divorces, and your issues become larger. When you leave a marriage for whatever reasons (remember everything takes two and **_no one person_** is totally to blame or be held responsible for a failed marriage), and unless you identify and deal with your issues and go into a new relationship baggage-free, you are going to have a difficult time to cope in the new one as well.

Here is a prime example of self-worth and esteem issues that can come and wreak havoc once again. This is because now you may feel like you are being compared to and comparing someone else to the previous spouse. You also have to work with another's children, more in-laws and extra things or issues you never knew were there. You had better be healthy and contented with where you are instead of choosing to embark on yet another relationship journey. Just sayin'…

You were created to be re-conciliators, you are to be peace keepers everywhere possible, you are even called to be ambassadors representing our Lord everywhere you go, especially in the family unit. Does that sound like the itinerary of a person with low-self-esteem?

I, (Your name)_____, declare that I will honor my mother, father, spouse and children as Christ honors and loves the church, His body; and my neighbor as myself.

NOTES

Chapter Six
Overcomers

Let your walk speak your talk!

"And they overcame him (the enemy of their souls, Satan) because of the blood of the Lamb AND the Word of their testimony..." - Revelation 12:11

"...thus says the Lord to you: 'Do not be afraid nor dismayed because of this great multitude, for the battle is not yours, but God's. Tomorrow go up against them... - 2 Chronicles 20:15

"For as the body without the spirit is dead, so faith without works is dead." -James 2:26

You go to countless seminars and conferences looking for a painless cure by which your life can be zapped and changed into the perfect "10". You may go on a diet, or join a health club, your enthusiasm runs strong for two or three weeks, maybe even a couple months, then oops...you fall back into the same old, same old plight.

The problem with programs and self-help agendas is they tell us what to do but can never give us the "**power**" to do it. You are given all sorts of useful information, but how do you do it? Where do we get this power to change? This power comes from the resurrection power that raised Jesus from the dead, and it is this power that is available to change your life here and now. The most important thing in life is knowing Christ and experiencing the power of His resurrection. Through Him, you can break the chains that bind you and the limits that constrain you, so that you can walk victoriously in His power today. (See Invitation at back)

Paul writes in Philippians 3:10, *"I pray that you will begin to understand how incredibly great His power is to help those who believe Him."*

You were not born that way...The book of Mark, chapter 3 tells us that Jesus came upon a man with a "withered hand." The Greek word *"xeraino"* translated "withered" means "to become dry, wasted away, or exhausted, drained of life."[10] This definition tells us that the condition of the man's hand was the result of an accident, some kind of disease, or influence of some sort from the _outside_. In other words, he wasn't born that way! Let me stop here and tell somebody here and now, yes, you, the one reading this book, _you_ weren't born that way!

You _weren't born_ depressed or angry, You _weren't born_ discouraged or fearful and lonely. You, a beautiful person, _were not born_ full of doubts about your future. You _weren't born_ with a broken heart and most certainly not with aborted dreams and lost visions. *You _weren't born_* to live disappointed and afraid of failures, unable to make decisions. But, life happened, just as it does to all of us at one

---

10   W.E. Vine, *Vine's Concise Dictionary of the Bible*, Nelson Reference & Electronics, 2005

time or the other, we live in a world (*that without the influence of our Creator has become a place of sorrow, since Adam and Eve sinned, dominion was turned over to the devil. That dominion was for us to use to promote the kingdom of God on this earth and Adam gave it away.*

GOOD NEWS, at the cross Jesus got it back. He is waiting for you to ask for it and to begin to live the kind of life intended for you, a blessed and victorious life in the presence of our God. Really, life is not always kind...and it's certainly not always fair. And now it has withered, exhausted and eroded and wasted your hand of faith...your expectations of better days.

Now you have stopped dreaming, stopped reaching, and stopped expecting. Like this man...you've just settled down into an existence. One of the worst things that can ever happen to a person is to just settle - no more movement, activity, and drive.

That withered hand represents all the negative elements in your life that contradict the promises of God; all the opposition to your dreams, visions and desires. Listen to me...you are NOT destined to live a withered life. You were made for more. You were made to THRIVE, and not just SURVIVE!

Jesus said to that man, "Stretch forth your hand." He can turn a withered life into an abundant life...if you just stretch. Go after it! Separate from the pack! And if somebody looks at you funny, just say, "<u>Excuse my reach</u>...but I see something God promised me...and I have to stretch to get it."

Be encouraged with this next wonderful quote by an awesome friend and huge man of faith: "When the voice of your accuser (the devil), or your symptoms, or your circumstances seem to be so loud, you can't stand it, turn up the volume of His Word inside you. If you can't seem to go there for one reason or the other, turn up the volume on praising Him, with thanksgiving. You can even begin to sing this song; I can see clearly now, the rain is gone, no obstacles in my way…"[11]

"When you pass through the waters, I will be with you; and through the river, they shall not overflow you. When you walk through the fire, you shall not be burned nor shall the flame scorch you. **- Isaiah 43:2**

When you find yourself looking in your rearview mirror and the only things you see are failure in your job, your marriage, as a parent or in your business, remember, Satan (referred to as the accuser of the brethren) hopes and in fact desires that you never open your Bible and read these words:

"The Lord upholds all who fall, and raises up all who are bowed down." **- Psalm 145:14 and 146:8b**

God will never, ever consult your past to determine your future. I've said it once, I will say it again, The Almighty God is fully aware of your problems, BUT He is also very much

---

[11]   Jim Christian, Senior Pastor of Christ the Answer International MInistry

aware of your potential. He made you and He planned for you to succeed!

The woman at the well went looking for love in all the wrong places. When Jesus found her, she already had five ex-husbands and a live-in boyfriend. She was the main course for gossip and would have been a tabloid's dream. Jesus told her, "whoever drinks of this water that I shall give him will never thirst (for meaning or significance) again. The water that I shall give him will become in him a fountain of water springing up into everlasting life." Paraphrased from **John 4:13-14**

And what did she say;

"Give me this water, that I may never thirst." v15.

Why don't you make this part of your daily prayer?

When physical scars heal, they usually leave a deformity of some kind as a reminder. Even these fade with time. Heart scars are a little different, and trying to heal them is much like putting a band aid on a bullet hole.

It doesn't matter where the scars come from, you are the only one who knows your scars well, who cut you, the circumstances, probably even date and time. Your particular abuse could have carried on for years or just a one-time episode, it doesn't matter, they are there nonetheless. Whether they are few or many, cuts and scrapes can become infected, they will begin to decay and stink up your life, they will begin to define you, limit you in life and particularly create a distrust of God. After all, He is supposed to know everything and stop the bad stuff from happening, right? Physical scars don't always cause pain, but heart scars do. My point is this: Jesus understands scars! [12]

> *There was nothing attractive about Him, nothing to cause us to take a second look. He was looked down on and passed over, a man who suffered and knew pain first hand. One look at Him and people turned away. We all looked down on Him, thought He was scum. But the fact is, it was our pains He carried – our disfigurements, all the things wrong with us. We thought He brought it in Himself, that God was punishing Him, for His own failures. But it was yours and my sins that did it to Him, that ripped and tore and crushed Him – our sins! He took the punishment, and that made us whole. Through his bruises we got healed.* -Isaiah 53:2-5 [13]**MSG**

Scars, both external and internal, are inevitable in every one of our lives, the difference will be what you do with those scars. You can use them to continue in a destructive lifestyle of self-pity, condemnation and guilt, or you can turn those scars over to Jesus and then use them to lift others up to victory and out of defeat, just as He did with His scars, HE made you whole!

---

[12]   Charles Stanley, *In Touch, monthly devotion*, March 2015
[13]   Eugene E. Peterson, The Message Translation, NAVPRESS, 2005

Pray this prayer whenever you need encouragement – paraphrased from Isaiah 61:3

Father, I, (Your name)_____declare that You have delivered me from the spirit of fear, and the lying spirit. I am no longer ashamed. Neither will I be perplexed and confused or depressed. You have given me beauty for ashes, the oil of joy for mourning, and the garment of praise for the spirit of heaviness, that I might be a tree of righteousness, the planting of the Lord, that You might be glorified. I, (Your name)_____ speak out in psalms, hymns and spiritual songs, offering praise with my voice and making melody with all my heart to the Lord for His grace and goodness to me. I encourage myself in the Lord every day, all day long. Praise You Lord. Amen

NOTES

Chapter Seven
Reach Out

"And as you would like and desire that men would do to you, do exactly so to them" - **Luke 6:31**

"And you shall love the Lord your God with all your heart, with all your soul, with all your mind, and with all your strength...and you shall love your neighbor as yourself." – **Mark 12:30-31**

"But I say to you, love your enemies, bless those who curse you, do good to those who hate you, and pray for those who spitefully use you and persecute you," - **Matthew 5:44 and Luke 6:28**

Unless you pour out what you have learned, you will not be able to receive more. It is like a river, there is always fresh water coming in from some source, the river must empty itself regularly or it will overflow its banks and won't be able to channel its flow or control it.

I encourage you to take what you have learned and to use it to help others like yourself to stretch themselves and reach for the stars.

How do you know you were not born for such a time as this to accomplish great things for the kingdom and thus for yourself, right here, right now.

Become encouragers to those who are still muddling through the storms that you just came through. Give them hope as you received hope, help them to dream and set goals. Then follow through step by step. Surround yourself and those around you with positive God-fearing people who will help you achieve the goals you have set for yourself according to the plan God has established for you.

I was not released from my mental prison until I felt the threat and potential sting of nearly losing my marriage, my sanity and my life. It took this huge reality to make me realize that I had to do something and do it now. I had been sexually abused as a very young child and this opened doors to demonic oppression in my life and it took its toll. I never felt free to be who I thought I should be, because of a spirit of fear instilled in me by my abuser who made me believe that if I told anyone, it would result somehow in the death of my mother. And of course my mothers' health was rocky in those days, so I believed every word. Thank God, she is still with us and is enjoying a full life at 84 years of age. Not until one day the Holy Spirit came to me and said if you don't begin to forgive, you will always be bound, chained to the lies. Every part of me screamed no, there has to be another way, I want him to pay for this...yada, yada. Thank the Lord, His Spirit was persistent and kept chipping away and chipping away until one day, I put one foot in front of the other and determined to set myself and my abuser free. Lo and behold, it did nothing for him. But did I lose 1000 lbs of guilt, shame and every other thing that had attached itself to me? I was no longer bound by the condemnation, the lies, playing re-runs in my head. Jesus was my only way to freedom.

This was not my only issue and hang up...I used food as my comfort and consolation, these old habits were harder to break than my cycle of hatred. My flesh was always (and at times still tries to tell me what it wants and how it wants it and how much it needs to be satisfied). At one time, it was constantly screaming out, feed me, stop the hunger, stop the pain, and it used to control every other decision I had to make. My friends, there are consequences to every decision we make. Choose wisely which voice you will heed. This is the same for every vice; drugs, alcohol, sex, gambling, food, porn, workaholics and shopaholics. When we chose something contrary to what is right, peace and health and the truth found in God's Word, when we make anyone or multiples of these things gods in our life, we will reap heartache, we will reap a negative outcome, which will inevitably bury us deeper in our pain. Our guilt will assault us with an aura of vengeance and the self-condemnation will torment us insatiably.

The good news is; Jesus experienced everything that is common to human trials and temptations and He overcame, you too can become free of the demons that plague you with fear and condemnation if you just turn it over to Him.

So with that said, I will recap: You know you have an issue with self-esteem, you should decide to do something about it NOW. You enlist a trustworthy friend(s) and you get yourself armed with some good material that has potential, now you

- Ask the Holy Spirit to help guide you.

- Ask the Lord to give you strength, courage and wisdom.

- You begin to write your issues down, (one at a time works best).

- You open up your Bible and concordance and begin to search for the meaning of terms that describe your condition.

- Once you find the scriptures you are looking for, begin to read till the Spirit identifies one or more for you and your situation, then ask what you are to do, sometimes He will say nothing, but is working it out for you.

- Begin to read and repeat out loud what it says about you and what He promises to help you break the strongholds.

- Practice saying the answer to yourself over and over till it rises up on the inside of you like a flood (now would be the appropriate time to do a happy dance); you are beginning to overcome the negative with the truth.

- Reward yourself when you succeed and don't be too hard on yourself when you don't, just keep pressing in, DON'T QUIT!

- Write these little nuggets on pieces of paper and put them all over your house where you will see them regularly and repeat them to yourself

- I will guarantee you a change if you faint not. Now go out and help someone else. Remember where you came from and don't be snared by the trap of the enemy's lies again.

Armed with all of what you have learned, you will need the armor as I promised earlier. You must learn what every piece of armor is, what it is for and how to use it.

The armor is used to resist the enemy whenever he attacks, and when it is all over, you will still be left standing.

To do this, you will need the strong **belt of truth** (knowing that God is truth, He doesn't change, He doesn't lie, and you must know the truth about what He thinks of you, whose you are and how much He loves you, the assurance of His promise to you, and your eternal life), the belt is the one piece of armor that all other pieces are hung from, without truth, you have no armor; and then the **breastplate of God's righteousness**, this *rightness with God* is not of our own but the righteousness of the blood of Jesus. Wear **shoes** that are able to speed you on as you **share the Gospel of peace** (standing firm in what you know is the truth about the Gospel or good news of the Scriptures and that when we accept Jesus' sacrifice on our behalf, we become brand new creatures). In every battle, you will need **faith as your shield** (if your faith and trust are not firmly grounded in the truth of God's Word regardless of what you see and feel and hear to the contrary, you will not overcome) to stop the fiery arrows aimed at you by Satan. You will also need the **helmet of salvation** (knowing full well that once you are reconciled as a child of God, nobody can snatch you out of His hand) and the **sword of the Spirit** (this is the most valuable weapon, you use the Word of God to slice and dice everything the enemy throws your way, you can confidently say, "It is written, Satan, get thee behind me") which is the Word of God. And as I like to call it the **lance of prayer** (because, prayer strategically placed can hit a target a long way off, you can knock your enemy to the ground before he can get near you) to remind God of His promises to you and the covenant promises to Christians everywhere. This armor becomes your best artillery in your battle, it is developed by faith and trust in the One who created you to be the best.

Psalm 91 is a perfect example of the most beautiful promise God made to you and I. If you come to Him in obedience and repentance and live your life according to His plan for you, there is nothing He won't do for you.

"You who sit down in the presence of the Most High God

spending the night in the shadow of El Shaddai

say this "God, you are my refuge

I trust in You and I am safe!

That's right – He rescues you from hidden traps,

He shields you from deadly hazards.

His huge outstretched arms protect you -

under them you are perfectly safe; His arms fend off all harm.

Fear nothing – not wild wolves in the night

not flying arrows in the day,

not disease that prowls through the darkness,

nor disaster that erupts at high noon

even though others succumb all around

drop like flies right and left no harm will even graze you.

You'll stand untouched, watch it all from a distance

watch the wicked turn into corpses

yes, because God is your refuge, the Most High your very own home

evil can't get close to you, harm can't get through the door

He ordered His angels to guard you wherever you go.

if you stumble, they'll catch you, their job is to keep you from falling

you'll walk unharmed among lions and snakes,

and kick young lions and serpents from the path.

If you will hold on to Me for dear life, says God

I'll get you out of any trouble, I'll give you the best of care

if you will only get to know and trust me.

Call me and I will answer, be at your side in bad times

I'll rescue you, then throw you a party

I will give you a long life and a long drink of salvation."[14]

I, (Your name)_____ will reach out to help my brothers and sisters and comfort them in the same way that Christ has comforted me. I will give even a cup of cold water in His name to those who need it.

[14]   Eugene E. Peterson, *The Message Translation*, NAVPRESS, 2005

NOTES

Chapter Eight

Paint The Barn, Ladies

"Mirror, mirror on the wall, what can I change to make it worth it all?"

"Turn your eyes upon Jesus, look full into His wonderful face and the things of this world will grow strangely dim in the light of His glory and grace."

This chapter is about the outward, physical self that people see and interact with every day. They don't know what you are experiencing inside and frankly my dear, most of them don't give a damn. People see what they see and draw their own conclusions about you as a person by what they witness and it becomes their first impression of you!

It is written that it takes only 30 seconds to make a lasting impression, make it a good one; because it may take a lifetime to change that impression.

Whether you believe it or not, the first-thirty-second encounter that people have with you will establish a preconceived perception or first impression that stays with them for a long, long time. What will that be?

There are things we can do on the outside that will minimize the damage of first impressions and take us through until we are transformed into the person we are striving to become.

I will make a list of the most important areas that need our constant attention and what you should do to maintain them.

- *Hair* - you may not always be able to have or afford the latest style or color, but you can keep your hair neat and clean. Try wearing a hairstyle that is complementary to your facial features. Something that is easy to maintain on a daily basis.

- *Attire* – Again, you may not be in the position to have the latest fashions and wardrobe. But what you do have can go a long way when it is properly taken care of. Wash your clothes regularly, press them if they need it and mend any items that are damaged. Many of our fashions today are very easy to maintain, so be aware. Accessories go a long way to changing the look of an outfit with much less expense, learn to choose your clothes carefully, especially color coordination, complexion and hair complementing and versatility with existing pieces already in your closet.

- **Posture** – This is always an indicator of how well we see ourselves. Stand tall and straight, sit straight, don't slouch, (as part of good health habits, do not cross your legs, for circulation purposes). Sitting correctly not only helps you to stay alert, but prevents back and neck discomfort.

- **Eyes** – As they say, eyes are the window to the soul. This is amazingly true. Always, always, always maintain eye contact. This is crucial to developing a hugely positive attitude about your self-worth and image. Your eyes also tell a lot about the status of your overall health. Do not wear sunglasses inside or when you are speaking to someone, remove them.

- **Hands** – **A**lways shake hands with people you are introduced to, with a firm and positive pressure, one or two pumps and you are good to go, please don't linger or touch unless you are well acquainted. Maintain your nails and skin with a good manicure and use lotion as much as needed. Life has a way of depleting our natural moisture and no one wants to shake hands with something that feels like sand paper to touch. Well-manicured hands usually catch my eye before anything else - that's me.

- **Hygiene** – Good personal hygiene is crucial. I don't want to smell you before I see you…showering and deodorant, a must, and not just weekly. Feet…look after your feet, if you are on them a lot, even if you aren't, take care of them, they have to (as all your other body parts) last you a lifetime.

- **Conversation** – Make sure you show people you appear interested in what they have to say, by occasionally nodding, develop the art of listening more than speaking, an occasional "yes", "mmmmhmhm", a simple "no" or even a raised eyebrow can show them you care and are still in tune with the conversation.

- **Look** - Look people in the eye when you are speaking to them and watch them as they speak to you. Don't look at your watch, don't turn away in the middle of a sentence, and don't interrupt! Excuse yourself if you have to leave, but wait till there is a break in the flow. Try to become knowledgeable about a few things so as not to appear, clueless. The world does revolve, even if it isn't around us all the time. Right ladies?

- **Over-all-health** - Nutrition, limit the intake of processed, fast foods, try to eat natural, organic as much as possible, limit your intake of high amounts of sugar, refined flour, ie; pasta, rice and baked goods, increase fish and chicken, and also limit red meats to a couple times a week, (preferably 3 oz. serving). Learn to cook healthy, exercise at least three times a week. The very best way to do this is to walk. Sleep* a minimum of 8 hours a night and drink at least eight 10-oz glasses of water per day. Decrease your intake of coffee, tea, and salt; try to eliminate all high sugar drinks (soda pop). Establish a regular routine of taking some time to relax for at least 15 minutes during a hectic day. These are just a few suggestions which are *vital to your success* in overcoming low self-esteem and poor self-worth. *When you look good, you will feel good. When you feel good, you will look good.*

- **Your public persona** – If you act different in public than you do when nobody is watching, you might have some self-worth issues. You should strive to be the same in and out of the public eye, so that you don't appear to be something you are not. Do you go out in public dressed like a raga muffin, or do you slouch around all day in your PJ's, how about using the 'drive thru' because you are not dressed to appear in public, or you send someone else to get you something from the store because you can't be bothered to get ready.

When you are under the weather, (which should be seldom if you look after your personal self, diligently) it is understandable to have someone do your errands for you but not regularly. And one more thing, if you are speaking with someone, eye contact is crucial. Don't look down, side to side or anywhere but right at the one you are talking to.

*NOTE – Sleep is extremely, extremely important. If you are not getting at least 8 hours of quality sleep, you will eventually begin to experience problems with your appetite, your concentration, your health, your relationships, your energy levels and your work habits. So please don't play games with your sleep time, this is when your body takes time to rejuvenate, repair and heal itself. Most important thing for you to remember to aid you in winding down before going to sleep is, try shutting down your computer and your cell phone at least 1-2 hours before you retire, take a nice soothing soak in the tub and maybe a warm glass of milk or water to give you the feeling of sleepiness.

I declare that I, (Your name) _____ will always present myself as an ambassador for the kingdom. My outward appearance will reflect the position I represent. A reconciliator, a daughter/son of the King.

NOTES

Chapter Nine

Stop and Think About It!

I hear Him whisper...prophetically to you

"Now you are ready!"

"Deep lessons I have taught you. Wonderful truths I have imparted to you. I have revealed My heart to you over and over as you studied My word, My delightful one. The lessons you have learned along your journey have transformed your life, if you let them, so arise and ascend with Me, because now you are ready!"

"Nothing I have spoken to you has been in vain or gone to waste. Your heart has taken in truth as the thirsty ground celebrates the rain. Even the pain and frustration you have walked through was not without eternal purpose. I have glorified My name in the midst of it all. You have stood the tests and trials and remained faithful to My word. Now you are ready to come into a new place of power and authority. Arise!

So few truly lay their hearts before me so I can heal or trust Me and believe the words that I speak, but you, beloved, have done so. I will now trust you with new opportunities to bring Me glory. Take them, they are from Me. I AM opening a new door for you to come through, a door of influence will swing wide open before you. What I have taught you by My word, will make you a blessing to your family, friends and others. Speak the truth of My words and I will work with you and through you. The time has come, for now you are READY!"[15]

Did you know your birth was strategically planned by God so you would be living in this very time? Your exceptional great value is needed on earth at this time. Your existence was uniquely timed by God so that your life and your worship of HIM would have the greatest impact on the sphere of influence you have been placed in. He intentionally set you up to succeed.

I declare that the voice of my beloved is loud and clear in my ear and I hear what He says about me and others. I decree to act on what I hear my Lord saying to me.

---

[15]   Passion Translation – Broadstreet Publishing Group, 2013, Fair use guidelines.

NOTES

Chapter Ten

Conclusion

What will be the end of this?

-...And you should put on the new man, who was created by God in righteousness and in the purity of truth... - **Ephesians 4:24**

The power of gaining/developing confidence in life should be tempered with self-control and patience, because it can be used for positive or negative, and thus be wary and careful not to use it for self-aggrandizement, as such, it looks, feels and acts like arrogance. As you gain confidence, think and use it wisely.

Having a Christ-centered confidence (trusting completely in the Lord, because you know you can't do it on your own, not by any stretch of your imagination) brings multitudes of blessings, including spiritual growth, personal achievement, peace and influence in areas around you, with friends, family, co-workers and strangers. When you rest in God's assurances for you, you become capable of accomplishments far greater than anything you can imagine.

Did I ever once imagine I would be writing anything, let alone a book? Not in this lifetime, yet by the grace of God, here we are – by HIS power in me, I wrote it and you are reading it. My prayer is that if even one of you will get something out of it to encourage major change in your life, I will have accomplished what the Lord gave me to do.

English, literature and composition or language arts were my worst subjects in high school.

When you begin to step out in complete trust of the Lord and what HE is telling and showing you by HIS word, everyone who knows how you were before will see and hear and witness a tremendous difference in you. The best way to draw near to those promises is to read them, write them down and then go to prayer for them to manifest in your life.

A bit of advice for you my friend, when you make a quality decision to seek God's guidance in the decisions before you, **you will** experience opposition to your reading time and your prayer time. You will notice that you will be assaulted by every distraction you can name and a few you didn't even think of.

As of this writing, I have three situations that need a lot of time, prayer and possibly fasting to bring to the forefront the direction I must take, when, what and how to proceed. Guess what? _DISTRACTIONS_ begin to assault my mind, my time, and my determination to do what I know has to be done, today, now. I know that the choice is mine whether to succumb to them or stick to praying and waiting on God. Here's a prayer you can use:

"Father God, far too often I try to mask the burdens and weight of my sinful flesh, with outward activities that seem good but are just distractions, forgive me. Help me to set aside the things that keep me from running the good race you have placed in front of me. I thank you in Jesus' name for setting my feet to the course. Amen. **Hebrews 12:1.**

The bottom line is this: Who we become and what we accomplish are predominantly results of how and what we think. What we think is due in large to how we see ourselves and what we feel about ourselves. If this is based on what is true, then we will learn to see our real *self* as God sees us. If we perceive to see ourselves according to how we think others feel towards us, we will get into the rut of looking at our self critically through the eyes of others. These can be good thoughts _or_ as we used to say in addiction counseling, a product of **stinking thinking.**

You will respond to the kind of thoughts you have – so my question to you is this: What kind of thoughts do you have about yourself and who is guiding your thought process – God or the world?

These are two diametrically opposing systems.

The Lord, when allowed control of the steering wheel of your thoughts, grants us the ability to think rightly no matter what challenges we face. Guarding yourself against worldly influence must be deliberately chosen and diligently maintained, and then developed through the words of our confession. (The words we speak through the day.)

A renewed mind begins with a surrendered life to the Lord. He must have full authority over your thoughts; if not, you will have no power to clear out the stuff that clutters and clouds and skews your thinking towards yourself and others, which in turn hinders you from living the full life He has ordained for you, here and now. What we think goes into our heart and eventually flows from our mouths. So consider carefully what you think.

NOTES

Chapter Eleven

What Does God Say About Who(se) You Are?

Scripture prescriptions. Take them as many times a day as needed.

Practical things that you can put into practice in your everyday life and have victory over the thoughts the enemy tries to plant in your heart and mind.

LET'S LOOK...Each phrase will be put in first person singular, you can use it whatever way makes you comfortable. I do encourage you to do your own investigations to see what scriptures work best for your individual situation. The Scriptures of the Bible being the inspired Word of God, are profitable for doctrine, for reproof, for correction, for instruction...so the man/woman of God may be complete and thoroughly equipped for every good work. It has the answers to all your problems and to all the issues you will face. Give it a go and turn it over on to Him. His word says,

Come to Me, all you who labor and are heavy laden, and I will give you rest. (Matthew 11:28)

    <u>1)</u> <u>Toxic thought</u> - you are worthless and will never amount to anything.

Scripture - *But all who have received Him—those who believe in His name—He has given the right to become God's children.* (John 1:12)

You declare – "I am a child of God. I am an heir with Jesus. I am a child of the King!"

> **2) Toxic thought** – I am stupid, everyone thinks I am, so I must be, I will never learn anything, I will never change.

Scripture – *He is the reason you have a relationship with Jesus Christ, who became for us wisdom from God, and righteousness and sanctification and redemption.* (1 Corinthians 1:3a; 2:16; and Philippians 4:13)

You declare – "I have the mind of Christ, and in Him I have wisdom, righteousness, sanctification and redemption. I can do all things through Christ who strengthens me!"

> **3) Toxic Thought** – I am confused, I don't know what to do or where to turn, every time I try something, it goes wrong. Why should this be any different?

Scripture – *But thanks be to God who always leads us (me) in triumphal procession in Christ and who makes known through us (me) the fragrance that consists of the knowledge of Him in every place.* (2 Corinthians 2:14)

You declare – "God always leads me in triumph and knowledge of Christ! I am a winner!"

> **4) Toxic Thought** – I (you) will never amount to anything, You are a loser…

Scripture – *There is neither Jew nor Greek, there is neither slave nor free, there is neither male or female – for all of you are one in Christ Jesus.* **(Galatians 3:28)**

You declare – "I am somebody. In Christ, we are all equal. I can do all things through Christ because I am blessed."

> **5) Toxic Thought** - What makes you think your special and that God loves you, who do you think you are, to act better than us?

Scripture – *Blessed is the God and Father of our Lord Jesus Christ, who has blessed us (me) with every spiritual blessing in the heavenly realms in Christ.* **(Ephesians 1:3)**

You declare – "I am chosen, holy and blameless before God!"

> **6) Toxic Thought** – Why would God listen to you, why would He answer your prayer, why would you think He would love someone like you (me)?

Scripture – *In Christ, we too have been claimed as God's own possession, since we were predestined according to the one purpose of him who accomplishes all things according to the counsel of His.* **(Ephesians 1:11)**

You declare – "I have Jesus in my life and I am sealed with the Holy Spirit of promise."

> **7) Toxic Thought** – Who do you think you are, after the kind of life you've lived?

Scripture – *And He raised us up with Him and seated us with Him in the heavenly realm. And in Jesus we are seated at the right hand of the majesty in heaven,* (Ephesians 2:6 and Luke 22:69)

You declare – "I am God's workmanship created to produce good works."

8) **Toxic Thought** – How do you know any of this is true?

Scripture – *...the Gentiles (heathens, unbelievers) in the new covenant are fellow heirs, fellow members of the body, and fellow partakers of the promises of Christ Jesus (in and through acceptance of Him)* (Ephesians 3:6; and Galatians 3:28-29)

You declare – "I have boldness and confident access to God because of Christ's faithfulness."

There are answers for every toxic thought you have, and you will find them in Scripture. I will give a few more, but the best is when you can find the ones that work for you, then meditate on them till they take root in your heart.

9) **Toxic thought** – worry, anxiety, depression

Scripture - *And the peace of God that surpasses all understanding will guard your hearts and minds in Christ Jesus* (Philippians 4:7)

You declare- "The peace of God guards my mind and heart at all times."

10) **Toxic Thought** – where is the money going to come from to pay the rent this month or the Dr. bills?

Scripture – *And my God shall supply your every need according to his glorious riches in Christ Jesus* (Philippians 4:19)

You declare – "God supplies all my *needs!*"

11) **Toxic Thought** – So what you gonna do with all this information, it's not true and just stupid, just think about how hard you are gonna have to work, what about the money you wasted for this book, for what?

Scripture – *Therefore, as the elect of God, holy and dearly beloved, clothe yourself with a heart of mercy, kindness, humility gentleness, patience and self-control.* (Colossians 3:12).

You declare – "I have been chosen by God, I am holy and loved."

Your real enemies are not people in and of themselves. What they appear to do to us is likely motivated by unseen forces beyond what you can see and hear in the natural realm. Seriously folks, there is a spiritual side to everything before there is a natural manifestation. Your battles are in the spiritual realm. There is a spiritual side that determines what happens in the natural.

So instead of shunning, blaming or getting upset with those who seem to hurt or scar us – forgive, love and pray for them – it may not do much for them initially, (I assure you that your prayers for them will not go unanswered) but it sure will lift a ton of weight off of your shoulders – when the burden is lifted, the load becomes less; and the lighter you walk, the better you will be able to handle difficult situations with a different attitude.

Entertaining certain thoughts, some of the choices you make, and your actions may yield to the influence of the realm of darkness OR they will likely cause you to lean towards God's purposes, ways and will.

Friend and author, Delaine Allen, writes: "We must rise up into a no-excuse living, keeping faith and good conscience as bold women of God."[16]

Guard against passivity and distraction, they both lead to destruction. **Proverbs 1:32**

Remember, although not easy, moving from victim to victor is up to you, entirely your choice to make, you are the only one who can make it – warning – just because you make a choice doesn't mean anything will change until *you put your choice into action,* and of course, *you cannot change other people,* but you can change how you react to them.

Giving up is easy but will you be happy, will you feel good about yourself?

Arise, shine; for thy light is come, and the glory of the LORD is risen upon thee **(Isaiah 60:1).**

---

[16]   Delaine Allen, *Women At War*, Worldwide Publishing Group; Houston, TX.. 2015, Pg 29.

If ye then be risen with Christ, seek those things which are above, where Christ sitteth on the right hand of God.

Set your affection on things above, not on things on the earth.

For ye are dead, and your life is hid with Christ in God.

When Christ, who is our life, shall appear, then shall ye also appear with him in glory **(Colossians 3:1-4).**

My friend, you are not a servant or a slave, but a royal daughter/son of your heavenly Father. You were created to demonstrate His dominion and authority here on earth (your purpose) and to give Him all the glory as you help build His kingdom on earth as it is in heaven – the Word of God is our sword and a strategic weapon in our arsenal for the battle before us.

For the weapons of our warfare are not carnal, but mighty through God to the pulling down of strong holds; Casting down imaginations, and every high thing that exalts itself against the knowledge of God, and bringing into captivity every thought to the obedience of Christ **(2 Corinthians 10:4).**

Take charge of your life, take charge of your self-esteem, know what you are worth to your heavenly Father and step into the battle as a victor and not a victim.

NOTES

#1 Extra prayer for those who struggle with depression –

Father, Your Word says that we should bring You into remembrance of the promises You have made to Your children, well, Lord, I am reminding You that You said You were my refuge and my high tower and my stronghold in times of trouble. You are my Father. Now I know that I am armed and dangerous to the enemy of my soul, the one who wants me to stay down and not rise up. Because I no longer perish for lack of knowledge and I can lean confidently and put all my trust in You, for You will never leave me or forsake me. I will always seek You as the final authority. I praise and thank You for Your unfailing love towards me.

In Jesus' name, I loose my mind from wrong thinking patterns. I tear down strongholds that have protected false perceptions I have had about myself. I submit to You, Father, and resist the spirit of fear, the spirit of falsehoods, the spirits of discouragement, the spirits of self-pity and the spirits of depression. I will give no place to the devil by harboring resentment and holding onto anger, unforgiveness and offense against anyone. I surround myself with all that is good and pure and worthy and lovely. I will shout with a voice of deliverance from all the lies I have believed about myself and I will continue to be an overcomer by the word of my testimony and the blood of the Lamb. AMEN.

#2 A prayer for those who struggle with keeping a gate on their lips. Growing up, many of us were taught that if we couldn't say anything nice, we shouldn't say anything at all. That's still good advice. Not only when we speak of others, but also when we speak of ourselves.

– based on Psalm 141:3, and Proverbs 13:3

"Set a guard, O Lord, over my mouth; Keep watch over the door of my lips."

"He who guards his mouth preserves his life. But he who opens wide his lips shall have destruction (problems)."

Father God, today I make a quality decision before You in the name of Jesus Christ. I turn from speaking idle words and foolishly talking things that are contrary to my true desire for myself and towards others. Your word says that the tongue defiles, that it sets on fire the course of nature and that the tongue is set on fire of hell. Therefore, I set my tongue apart to speak Your truth, not lies.

In the name of Jesus, I am submitting to godly wisdom so I might learn to control my tongue. I am determined that hell will not set my tongue on fire. Here and now, I reject and repent of every idle word that has ever crossed my lips. I cancel its power and dedicate my mouth to only speak excellent and right things. My mouth shall utter truth from this day forward.

Because You say that I am the righteousness of God in Christ, I set the course of my life for obedience, abundance, wisdom, health, wholeness and peace and joy in You, Lord. Set a guard over my mouth and a gate over my lips, so that the words of my mouth and the meditations of my heart would be pleasing in Your sight.

I purpose to guard my mouth and my tongue that I might keep myself from calamity.

Father, Your words are top priority to me, they are spirit and life. I will let Your word dwell in me richly in all wisdom. The ability of God is released within me by the words of my mouth. I speak, and they become alive and working in and through me. I can boldly say that my words are words of faith, words of power, words of love, and words of life. They shall produce good things in my life and in the lives of those I speak over. Thank You, in Jesus' name. AMEN.

#3 A prayer for those who struggle with the meditations of their hearts –

Father, Your word says that You desire truth in the inward parts; and in the hidden parts, You will make me to know wisdom. It also says that if I need wisdom, I can come and ask for it and You will give it to me liberally. Here I am, I am asking that You create in me a clean heart and renew a steadfast spirit within me, so that the meditations of my heart would be pleasing in Your sight and that out of the abundance of my heart, my mouth will speak in love and understanding. Thank You, Lord that You are faithful to answer my request when it is in line with Your will for me, I know this is in line with Your will. Praise You, Lord. Amen.

Be encouraged and don't give up, you are already a more self-confident person than you were before. How do I know this? You bought this book, with the intention of doing something about your low self-esteem, and here you are on the last few pages and already you are formulating plans, armed and ready for war, determined to put all of your new weapons to work for you.

Bless you and happy adventure as you break the mold!

Don't let the world around you squeeze you into its own mold, but let the Creator remold your mind's from within, so that you can prove in practice that the plan for your life is GOOD!

"Don't accept the world's views as the snapshot of who you are."

Instead, with your eyes wide open to the Creator's compassion, let His idea of you, shape your life and bring beauty and purpose out of the ashes.

Start now by the total changing of and renovation of your mind.

When we think our problems are too complex and that no one has experienced what we have, we put ourselves in a position of bondage and separation from those who also have gone through tough times and are willing to help and comfort you.

With this New Mind...which does not spring forth in a moment...it must be the choices of our everyday life.

Salmon swim against the current of a powerful river against all reason, because they have a goal to press towards. They are gripped from within with their true destiny and are supernaturally designed to reach it and propagate their kind. So are you!

Declaration

I, (Your name) _____can do all things through Christ's anointed power from within which strengthens me and helps me to press toward the mark of the High Calling on me.

I was not created for a low-life existence and to wander about with no purpose...I desire the full, abundant life paid for and by grace, I choose to live this life to the fullest, here and now! Amen!

Your Invitation,

...to the best, life has to offer, not just for eternity but here and now, that life is in Jesus Christ

There are many who still don't know and haven't asked Jesus to come into their life. I would like to encourage you to decide to get to know my Jesus personally. You can, by repeating this prayer with a truly repentant heart. When you are done, please share with someone or contact me, find a good church (that teaches the whole counsel of God), get a good Bible and begin to study and read and find out what awesome and wonderful things the Lord has in store for you as you begin your new journey as a brand new creation of Almighty God. Join a good Bible study and learn about the One who created you.

Pray this way...

LORD JESUS, I know I haven't been living the kind of life you wanted for me. I am sorry and ask for YOUR free gift of salvation, which includes forgiveness, deliverance and healing. I ask you, Jesus to come and live in my life. JESUS, I repent and promise to completely turn away from the old life that had me bound. I believe YOU lived life as an example for me, and YOU died in my place to restore my relationship with my Heavenly Father. I believe YOU rose again on the third day to give me the hope of eternal life spent in the Presence of the Lord. Save me now through your atoning blood shed on the cross for me. Amen and Thank You.

NOTES

About the Author

Sharon and her husband of 43 years, Edwin, currently reside on a farm near Prince Albert, Saskatchewan, Canada. Edwin is retired and enjoys fishing, gardening and looking after their yard. They have two adult children, Glenn, and daughter Alana.

Sharon graduated from Fountain of Life School of Ministry in 2003 and has pastored in various communities and as of 2008 is Senior Pastor of a small church (Way of Wisdom Ministries) in Prince Albert, Saskatchewan.

Her hobbies are reading, cooking and watching football in summer. Ministry doesn't usually leave a lot of room for extracurricular activities but Sharon and her husband always manage to do several BBQ's and show hospitality to whoever comes.

Sharon and Ed enjoy being part of mission trips and over the years have worked with other ministries in communities such as Fort Providence, NWT; Pangman, SK.; Kehewin First Nations, Red Earth First Nation, as well as Lima, Peru. Also they have assisted in fund raising for *Rays of Hope for Uganda*.

To contact them:

Rev. Sharon & Edwin Kühn

R.R. #3, STN MPP

Prince Albert, SK., Canada

S6V 5R1

1-306-961-7082

Email: <u>skuhn1@sasktel.net</u> *or FB messaging*

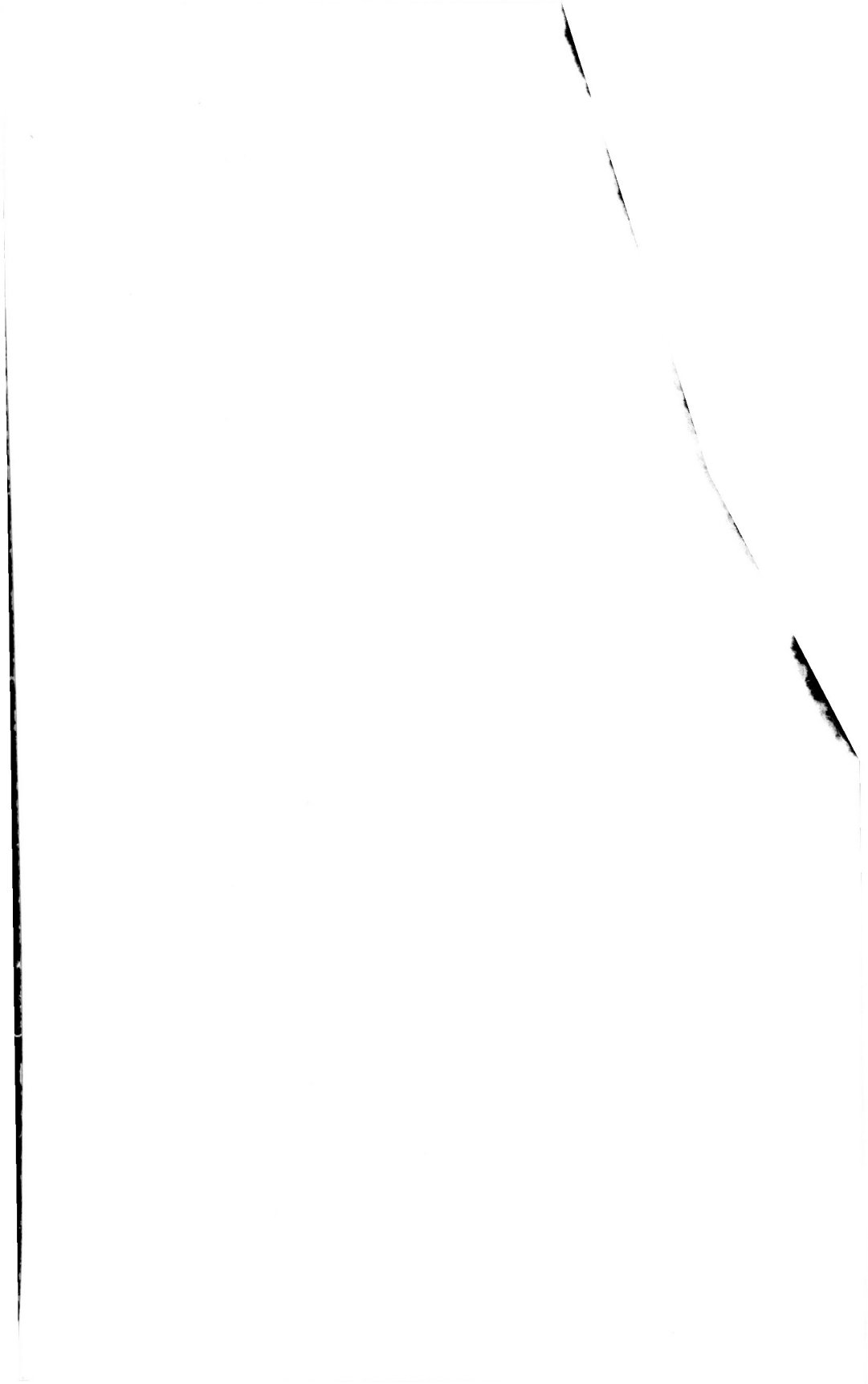

www.ingramcontent.com/pod-product-compliance
Lightning Source LLC
Chambersburg PA
CBHW021828090426
42811CB00032B/2072/J